MEMOIRS OF AN AMERICAN SAMURAI

A Modern Day Warrior's Journey Through The World Of Martial Arts!

GARY LEE

Compiled by

JAY VIKAZ

A MUSEUM OF SPORT KARATE PUBLICATION

Copyright © 2011 by **Gary Lee**

All Rights Reserved.

No part of this publication may be reproduced in any form or by any means, including scanning, photocopying, or otherwise without prior written permission of the copyright holder.

Liability Disclaimer

The author, publisher or compiler cannot be held responsible in any way for the information or content in this book. This book is intended purely for educational and entertainment purposes only

ISBN-10: 1463698062
ISBN-13: 978-1463698065

First Printing, 2011

Printed in the United States of America

Book Design by Jay Vikaz

Published By
The Museum Of Sport Karate
www.SportKarateMuseum.org

Quotes

"Gary Lee is the Voice of Karate."
- Michael Matsuda, President, The Martial Arts History Museum

"Gary Lee is the embodiment of the belief that one person can truly make a difference."
- Joe Corley

"He is a tireless worker for the Sport Karate History that should be told and shared."
- Karl E. Geis Black, Belt Magazine Hall of Fame, Kudon Judo, Kudon Aikido

"Professor Gary Lee is an old-timer and knows everyone! He shares with him an Aloha spirit from his homeland and he has a sense of humbleness, but lives as a samurai, poet, actor, artist, historian, and warrior."
- Erik D. Jones, Executive Producer, Martial Arts Exclusive

"Professor Gary Lee should be given tremendous credit for his extraordinary effort to create a Black Belt Museum. The martial arts museum will be an institution that provides inspiration to the entire martial arts world."
- Keith Vitali, Black Belt Magazine Hall of Fame

"Gary is a historian, a educator, an actor, an entertainer, a Samurai and a Big kid rolled up into one heck of a role model for kids, young adults and parents. There is no one I know who has the elite history he does in sport karate, after all he sold me back in 1982 to be the first martial arts show Astroworld had and helped create many shows after that year with fight scenes, high falls, tricks, weapons and comedy. The Hollywood Stunt Show was a big hit and Gary played the lead. Gary is like a Tsunami."
- Bob Logon, Entertainment Warner Brothers / Six Flags / Astroworld, Retired

Dedication

This book is dedicated to my partner, wife and best friend for thirty years, Tammy and the joy of my life, our son Garett who has changed my life and shown me that Karate is my way of life.

Acknowledgments

I would like to acknowledge the following persons (in no particular order) for their part in my continuing journey in the Martial Arts and for, without their love and devotion toward me, I could not have been able to bring this journey to life for all to read.

Jim Harrison, Ed Parker, Dana Carter, Tim Berg, Sheridan Beauving, Mike Hicky, Al Dacascos, Chuck Norris, Sid Campbell, Donald William Cross, Margret Cross, David O'kelly, Pete McAbee, Darrin Gazaway, Andrew Tamper , William Ping Hi, Sam Chapman, Jerry Piddington, Joe Corley, Lois Cross, Shirley Carlton, Larry Carlton, Al Lassitor, Brent Hunt, Professor Wally Jay, Al Garza, Jimmy Tabares, Kevin Roy, George Minshew, Robert Sanders, Dixie Sanders, Bob Logan , Jack Farr, Leo T. Fong, Steve Love, Don Smith, Roy D.Kurban, Ernie Radar Smith, Steve Fotenot, Twain Kennedy, Glen Kwan, Scott Holgath, William Oliver, Tadashi Nakumura, Kishi Sensei, Ted Tabura, Mike Stone, Mark Gerry, Art Commacho, Eric Lee, Rick Clunn, John Hunt, Dave Hazzard, Ishmael Robles, Dr. Maung Gyi, James Toney, Brian Duffy, Allen Steen, Duane R. Ethington, Tammy Sanders Lee, Keith Vitali, Mike Genova, Bruce Brutschy, Danny McCall, Ricky Smith, Flem Evans, Glenn Keeney, Parker Shelton, Bill Wallace, Dan Hect, Bill Viola, Fumio Demura, Joe Jennings, Century Martial Arts Fitness, Ken Knudson, Lee Barberito, Andrew Linick, Philip Bradley, Patrick McCarthy, United States Black Belt Hall of Fame, Dr.Dan Tosh, Patrick Price, Frank Dux, Adam James, Buddy Hudson, Robert Young, Barry Moyer, Bruce Hirsch, Zulfi Ahmed, Jamie Cashion, Aaron and Michelle Perzan, Angela Connelly, Bernie "Pops" Kransoo, Susan Andrade, Dan Jones, Dana Stamos, Daryl Stewart, Susie McDowell, Chuck McDowell, Eddie Morales, Robert Parham, Larry Lunn, Carl Geis, Joshua St.Ives, Jay Vikaz, Jeff Smith, Jimmie Jones, Michael DePasquale Jr., Michael DePasqwuale Sr., Jhoon Rhee, Kamrun Jenabzadeh, Keith Yates, Richard Jenkins, Breck Mills, Michael James, Outlaw Dave, Pat Johnson, Hale Hisabeck, Wade Kirkpatrick, Howard Jackson, Ray Skilleran, Al Hippert, Linda Denley, Young Song Lee and my lovely children Robin Shockley and Garett Lee.

If I have left some one out, it is not because I do not value what you have done, but only because my age must be catching up and my memory may be playing tricks on me. I will always cherish you in my heart.

About The Cover

This Handcrafted portrait by Hanshi Sid Campbell from the 1980's depicts Professor Gary Lee as a Samurai. Hanshi Sid Campbell was Professor Gary Lee's instructor, friend and mentor.

This portrait has been incorporated in the book cover design to honor Hanshi Sid Campbell and because it represents the Samurai spirit that Professor Gary Lee embodies. In a way, the title of this book was inspired by this portrait, when Jay, the compiler of this book, learned about the history and significance behind it.

TABLE OF CONTENTS

Acknowledgments vii

About The Cover ix

Foreword xiii

The Tale Of Forty Brooms 23

The Leo Fong Connection 33

Black Belt Television 45

The Draw 55

The Old Japanese Fisherman 63

Hawaiian Son – Texas Star 71

Thoughts From The Japanese Waterman 85

Four Fingers Of Death 93

What Does Not Kill You Makes You Stronger 97

The Apple Does Not Fall Far From The Tree 103

A Tale Of Two Sports 117

Bass Fishing Tournament – Karate Style 117

A New Beginning 131

Words From Legends And Peers 137

Documents And Certificates 147

Notes From My Diary 165

Foreword

He came to Texas and my Black Belt Academy schools in Houston as a young, wide-eyed purist with all his worldly goods in a knapsack. Gary had but one goal, to practice his art and expand his skills and knowledge to the exclusion of all else.

I wondered if this kid had the right stuff to make it in the rough and tumble world that was karate in Texas at the time. I decided to give him a chance and a job. Thus began a relationship and friendship that has spanned over 30 years. Gary met his beautiful wife Tammy, a student in our system, fell in love and married. They have been together ever since. Out of this union came another that would add to our story together, their wonderful and talented son Garett.

It has been my privilege to be instructor, mentor, coach and friend to the entire Lee family. Gary, Tammy and now Garett have honored me with the designation teacher with all that entails.

I have said many times that if there were no Gary Lee, the martial arts would have to invent one. Who else would/could take on the role of historian and curator for NO PAY?

Gary, you are a unique and special individual. Thanks for all you do.

George Minshew

Texas National Team
Chris Minshew, Jennifer Robles, Professor Gary Lee, Tony Lopez, Danielle Dixon

MEMOIRS

OF

AN AMERICAN

SAMURAI

*A Modern Day Warrior's Journey
Through The World Of Martial Arts!*

GARY LEE

Gary "Musashi" Lee

BUSHIDO
The Way of the Warrior

Chapter 1
The Tale Of Forty Brooms

The Tale Of Forty Brooms

The stories you are about to read are true and have been lived out by the Old Sensei. There are lessons to be learned at an early age and this is one of many.

I was nine years old and I had lived with Sensei now for three years on big WAKIKI. It was beautiful, a paradise for tropical wonders and man. The jungle, the beach and Martial Arts all blended into sort of a dream for me.

I had lost my parents when I was four years old and had to live with my uncle. He was a mean man and I didn't like him. One night he hit me and beat me for not taking out the trash and I decided to run away. He was always screaming. I think he missed my dad. I really believe he was forced to take care of me.

Well, of course I didn't go far before I was found and punished. I was told not to leave my little hut where I lived. You might say I was grounded without privileges.

Sand, ocean and jungle are not much for a six year old to do. Plus, I was extremely lonely and missed my parents. I remember sneaking out late at night, walking down to the huge ocean to sit at the edge of the water pretending to see the mainland and all the wonders I had read about in the magazines.

We had no television, not even a radio, but even then I had dreams that one day I would leave this beach and start my journey.

One night I couldn't sleep, so I went down to the beach and what I saw would change my life forever. In the ocean, late at night, in the crashing waves of

Waikiki, I saw my first real Karate. Groups of black belts were in the ocean doing kata underneath the moonlight.

I was overwhelmed and from that moment I knew what I wanted to be, a black belt, a REAL BLACKBELT.

The next morning I asked my uncle about the late night karate class. He was mad that I even knew about it. Nonetheless, I would go down to their workouts on the beach. I was only six years old and scared to death, but I knew this was my destiny.

I started to go everyday after school to the tiny little hut they called a dojo. No carpet, no mirrors, no air conditioning just a tiny hut, thirty foot by thirty foot in size with sand all around.

Soon, I was there every day and night. Then one day, Sensei Kishi told me I would be staying with him instead of my uncle. I really don't know all of the details, but Sensei would be training me and sending me to school. I guess I was traded for something, I never found out. Even on my uncle's deathbed he would not tell me.

Now I am training everyday and night studying Budo. The first real lesson you never forget and it stays with you forever. I had just finished my chores around the dojo and I wanted to go surfing with my friends. The wind had just picked up and the waves were breaking ten to fifteen feet off the north end of the shore. It was perfect!

I told Sensei Kishi I was done and I was going to go out in the water. He looked up at the sky and said, "No, bad weather coming, you not surf today, too dangerous, you stay and train."

Well, it was the first time I ever argued with him. I didn't really argue, I just kind of smarted off to him and said, "What? You don't surf. All you do is karate. I need a break every now and then you know. I'm sick of training. All I do is train."

It would be the last time, the only time I would ever raise my voice or smart off in a bad attitude to him again. Without hesitation or emotion Sensei Kishi said, "I want you to walk into town to the hardware store and see the manager, Mr. Williams. I need for you to pick up forty brooms and bring them back here before the storm comes."

I never saw Sensei look at me like he did that day. It was like I had done something I had never done before and he was teaching me a lesson. Of course, I didn't understand it at the time. I was mad because I could not go surfing and now I had to go pick up forty brooms in Honolulu, which was a ten-mile walk.

About half way down that sandy road to Honolulu I realized I didn't know how I was going to carry the forty brooms back from town. Then it happened. The loudest thunderclap I have ever heard and then the rain came down. It was hard rain.

I was so mad, I was crying. Why would he make me walk in a storm and why was I going to town to pick up forty brooms? I was so concerned with my own being, I had forgotten about the lesson.

The lesson was - Never question, just do and do without a bad attitude. Most of all it was about respect.

He knew the storm was coming and he knew I could have been killed in the waves. A couple of kids had drowned. He was just taking care of me like he had done for all these years. But still, what about the forty brooms?

I finally got to the hardware store, soaking wet and scared because I didn't know what to expect. Mr. Williams had received a phone call and was expecting me when I walked in the store. He had put duct tape around both ends of the handles of the brooms so I could drag them back to the dojo.

I could see Mr. Williams felt sorry for me. I was a big kid but I was only nine years old and a major storm had hit Honolulu. Mr. Williams said, "Kid, I will let you take the wheelbarrow. Just bring it back. I don't know what you did to make Sensei Kishi so upset!"

Well it helped a little but not a lot. Sand, rain, hard rain, a wheelbarrow and a kid pushing it for ten miles, well you can imagine. I was tired and mentally wasted. I cried a lot that day. I learned the lesson, never talk back and always respect your peers, but most important, never question or raise my voice to Sensei, for he is the teacher.

I finally got back to the dojo and was met by Sensei at the door. He looked at me and I broke down and cried again. I said I was sorry for my attitude and it would never happen again.

I believe that day changed my life. I can't remember ever getting upset since that walk in the rain. Sensei Kishi and I bonded that stormy day like father and son. Oh, by the way, what happened to the forty brooms?

That night Sensei Kishi demonstrated Kyoshi-Jujitsu. He gave the brooms one at a time to each blackbelt present. Then he instructed each blackbelt to attack him with an overhead or thrusting strike, broom handle forward.

What I saw next I have never seen again in my entire world travels. He broke the brooms in half. The punch from the arm symbolized the attacking blow. He was so precise that he would break it low symbolizing the wrist and then high which would be the elbow breaking.

He stopped at thirty-nine and said, "Gary get the last broom and bring it to me now!" I was so scared and it was so silent you could hear a pin drop on the sand. Remember there were over thirty black belts there plus all the students. No one knew what my day had been like or the lesson that I had learned, but that was okay because I did learn.

So, I took the last broom, got into attack position and waited for Sensei to "kia" for my attack.

I waited and waited. It seemed like forever.

He moved. I screamed and thrust the broom forward as hard as I could with my body and soul. He caught the handle, flipped it over, swept me to the floor and was sweeping my face and body in about three seconds from the time I had thrust the broom at him. Wow! He could have broken my arm and taken me out of the picture.

He helped me up, hugged me and we both said "Ous". For the very first time I realized what "Ous" meant. RESPECT, RESPECT, RESPECT!

Then he gave me the unbroken broom and said, "Gary you will not forget this day for I would like for you to sweep the front area of the dojo everyday after school until you leave."

The front of the dojo area was sand!

I took the broom and said, "Yes sir sensei." I swept the front area everyday until I was fourteen and left for the mainland.

When I left Hawaii in 1969 I had my blackbelt, a white gi, a 1969 Blackbelt Yearbook, a 5'8" cream Gorden and Smith Twin Fin surf board and that broken broom.

"Ous".

BUSHIDO
THE CODE OF THE SAMURAI

Be acutely honest throughout your dealings with all people.
Believe in justice, not from other people, but from yourself.
To the true Samurai, there are no shades of gray
in the question of Honest and Justice.
There is only right and wrong.

Chapter 2
The Leo Fong Connection

The Leo Fong Connection

I have gathered my Black Belts to watch the movie "KILLPOINT" a film that stars Mr. Leo Fong, a martial arts Living Legend. I just received it in the mail with an autographed cover. Mr. Leo Fong was one of my first heroes when I came to the mainland.

My students and I are looking forward to watching some of the best to be karate stars on screen like Steve "Nasty" Anderson and Linda Denley just to name a few but most of all, I have gathered my Black Belts to teach them a sport karate history lesson and talk to them about how I met this great martial artist – Leo Fong.

It is 1974 and I have been fighting in the mainland now for over five years and built a small reputation for being an all around type of competitor. In the seventies not many Black Belts did three divisions, fighting, kata and weapons. I wanted the respect and I decided to give it all and in my eyes it paid off. Black Belt judges were coming up to me asking who I was and where I was from. I would proudly say "HAWAII!"

I had not won a major event yet but I was placing seconds and thirds behind the top competitors of that time. Back then competition was fun and exciting – even losing was a thrill because you were building the legacy that would last a lifetime.

One of the first books I paid for as reference of knowledge was Leo Fong's now famous "Sil-Lum Kung Fu." What drew my interest: it was a soft style and it translates as "young forest" simply meaning to be able to be flexible and like a young tree, bend with the wind.

I was fascinated, it was just the opposite of what I have been told to do since I was a kid training in Hawaii - knock them down and go straight forward. Hit first, hit last, go for the knockout!!!

....evade, dodge, counterpunch, move in circles all the time.

I found an uki (partner) and starting practicing what was in the book.

It was new and it was fun!!

I had read the 1970 Black Belt Magazine article on Leo Fong's life and I was impressed with his attitude toward fighting and his background as a kid being subjected to racism and how he overcame the racist surroundings he was in.

I wanted to learn Sil-Lum but because of my traditional karate background, I was never in the kung-fu circles or around that atmosphere of teaching, so his book became my source of learning. I would practice all the techniques in my mind and with my uki. I was getting better with my hands and expanding my mind learning kung-fu.

It was a secret, only because back then you did one or the other. I remember one of my Shito-ryu buddies saw my worn out, beat up Sil-Lum book and started on me asking me all these questions. Like, why I'm fighting different lately? And why do you want to box all the time?

MEETING THE ALL-TIME GREATS!

Through conversations, I had heard the Black Belts talk about that Mr. Chuck Norris was forming a new karate League, THE UNITED FIGHTING ARTS FEDERATON LEAGUE and the first tournament was going to be in Ohio.

Where Is Ohio?

I had just been in the mainland a few years and never competed out of California. I heard Mr. Norris was bringing in some important judges and one of them was Leo Fong – and for some reason, I felt I needed to compete.

It would be my first out of state event since I moved to the mainland. In my mind if I could win an important event, in front of important judges, I would have the confidence I needed to work even harder to win the next event!

I had no car, no contacts and no money for a plane ride or bus. I decided to hitch hike cross-country. I drew a map of the destination, found the small town of Warren, Ohio (I believe that was the city) and started my journey on Thursday morning - leaving North Hollywood.

Back in the '70s, hitchhiking was sort of safe – I mean, a lot of people did it and I had no other way to get there. My only concern was time. I was taking a big chance. I had to be across country, four or five states, in two days and by 10:00AM Saturday morning for Black Belt Kata and weigh-in. I wish I knew then what I know now because I was passionate about sport karate and I made decisions from the heart and not the mind.

I really can't remember all the rides and super cool people I met. I do remember it took six rides from California to get to Ohio and that Saturday morning was real tough. Not only was I still far away from the event but it was snowing. I had never seen snow. I had not even carried socks with me, just my karate stuff and tennis shoes. I remember how cold it was: I was in a pain I have never felt before, it was so cold it hurt to breathe and I was running late.

THE REST IS SORT OF A BLUR!

1975 FIRST UNITED FIGHTING ARTS CHAMIONSHIPS, WARREN, OHIO

The man in the car thought I was nuts because I was screaming about the time. The event started at 10:00AM and it was 10:15 or 10:20 Saturday morning. God bless him – he took me to the doorsteps of the arena.

I ran to the ticket booth and asked if competition had started and I saw the answer with my own eyes. Mr. Norris was lining up all the Black Belt kata competitors and I did not want to miss that division – that was half the reason I hitchhiked out here (the other half was to fight).

I remember begging the lady to please send a note down to the floor to Mr. Norris to ask him to hold the division because I had hitchhiked from California to compete. The judges were already sitting down and I knew I had blown it.

The lady thought I was crazy – she almost called security until she realized that I was sincere. The lady took my note and gave it to a runner who took it down to Mr. Norris.

Those seconds between the runner taking the note and Mr. Norris saying I could compete were like hours; it was intense. Then I got the okay and they were waiting for me. I had to dress in the hall way and run down the steps in front of everybody.

I got to the floor and said thanks but then a lady came up to me and said "You have to go first!!"

Whoaaaaaaaaa! What happened to random order? Flip the cards? Well, because they had held up the division for me, I had to go first!

Okay, okay, I'm ready, this is what I came for, this is my ring and God brought me here for a reason!

I looked at the line up and I did not know any of the Black Belts. There were around twenty competitors. I am sure they were all great guys and good

Black Belts but in my heart, no one trained as hard as I did and I know no one hitchhiked to get there, but most of all I wanted this division really bad!

Then it happened, I looked at the judges and got scared to death, I mean I was really nervous. If I remember it right, sitting on the Black Belt board were Ted Volrarth, a Vietnam veteran who did spectacular self-defense demos around the world, and my childhood hero Al Dacascos - he is acknowledged for being the first kung-fu fighter in the blood and guts history of sport karate and his demos were awesome to behold, the hero of my kung-fu memories, Sifu Leo Fong, who had secretly taught me Kung-Fu through his book Sil-Lum and Aaron Norris, who was one the best point fighters ever but is mostly known for his stunt work in movies and TV (He would later become one of the best action directors in Hollywood).

It was the first time I saw Chuck Norris. He was special, you could tell by the way he walked and talked. I didn't even think about it until after the tournament but he could have said no instead of yes and I would not have had this story. I knew his history – he was a great fighter and warrior of the blood and guts tournament scene and he was a real champion. His eyes were what stood out to me and he had kind eyes.

These were the important judges I wanted but going first in this competition was a drag.

"Focus. Kime. Don't look at the people. Look at their combined history. Look at their knowledge. Tell them the story. Do the Kata the way you were taught in Hawaii and win or lose.

You did your best.

Focus. Focus. Focus."

THESE WERE THE THOUGHTS GOING THROUGH MY HEAD!!

I remember doing "OUS" and tying for third place out of twenty competitors. I came back and did a Japanese Kata NI JI SHI HO and won, taking third place. That was great after all I had been through.

I was still cold from that white stuff that I had never seen before (snow) and all that worry about getting there on time had stressed me out to the max but now I could do what I do best and that is fight.

I remember winning three fights and walking out with third place. I won the last fight with a dropped kick to the groin (now illegal in most karate circuits today). The techniques used in the seventies would devastate a lot of opponents today just because back then we meant to stop you with one technique and we trained very hard to learn that one punch or kick.

Our attitude as warriors was simple. I will buy you a coke, maybe lunch, heck, I will even buy you dinner but it is war when we step into the ring, with respect always. Respect had to be in the ring for the contact level was high and the classiest competitors had the control but could nail you at any time! Let's just say it was scrappy.

I still have those trophies today beaten, battered and broken. They were black and had a hologram design down the middle. They sit on my office wall and visitors come into my office and asked about those beaten tore up broken trophies. I just say it was a day that I met my heroes and just can not let them go. I guess I will keep them forever.

I stayed in Ohio one more day because I was so fascinated by the snow and the very cold weather. Sleeping in the greyhound bus station that night, I realized that I had gone to an extreme state of mind to be here and I wondered if the rest of my career was going to be as complicated as this adventure. The next morning, I packed the two third place awards in my duffle bag and before I headed back to California, I also stopped by a five and dime store to buy a pair of socks.

I didn't know how many states this snow would last and my feet were cold.

The year was 1982 and in America if you were a warrior, you were chasing those KARATE ILLUSTRATED MAGAZINE POINTS. I was still chasing those first places but now it was even harder: you had George Chung, John Chung, Cindy Rothrock, Peter Morales and a slew of other great performers who always took first in their respective divisions but the most excitement was always the GRAND CHAMPIONSHIP OF THE TOURNAMENT.

The GRAND did not give you points but what it got was the respect of the competitors. The unwritten law: they were the best at the event – period. No questions asked, decided by the best karate form judges in America. JOHN CHUNG was my personal favorite – I would get goose bumps watching him and then had to go out and compete against him (talk about pressure).

LEO FONG and RON MARCHINI would produce the TOP TEN NATIONALS in Stockton, California and I was living in Texas chasing points from all around the country. A few of the Texans were traveling too, like JIMMY "Gato" TABARES, AL FRANCIS, AL GARZA, and of course Living Legend LINDA DENLEY.

My very first sponsor was the Hilton Hotels and I was treated very well: first class airfare, entry fee paid, hotel room, food expense and clothing. I wore a little patch in front and Hilton in big letters on my back.

On the flight to Stockton, I met JEAN FRENETTE and this was his first karate tournament in America and his first national event ever. JEAN FRENETTE LATER BECAME ONE OF CANADA'S GREAT FORMS CHAMPIONS. He was so nervous, so I gave him all my best tips on winning and we became fast friends that weekend.

Mr. Marchini picked us up at the airport and was very kind to us. He even walked me to my room and carried my luggage for me – I was very impressed. Jean and I hung out at the bar telling war stories with the VIPs but Saturday morning it was all business.

Seeing Mr. Fong again was a delight. I don't know if he remembered me from back in 1975 but I just thought it was cool to be competing in his event. I lost to Jean Frennette and Cindy Rothrock that day and it was another hard fought third place. And I still have that short red Top Ten third place trophy next to my SIL-LUM book.

Well my next encounter with Mr. Leo Fong would be in 2005 in Tarzana, California. I had just finished performing at the BLACKBELT MAGAZINE FESTIVAL OF MARTIAL ARTS at UNIVERSAL STUDIOS-HOLLYWOOD.

After a couple of days, Adam asked us out to lunch, and he said he was inviting his instructor and World Champion John Chung and his wife. You will never guess who Adam's instructor was … MR. LEO FONG!!!!!!!!!!!!!!!!

I was excited that I would finally get to just talk to him, one on one and get to ask all the questions I've had bottled up all these years. He was very polite and I could feel his chi – it was strong. I felt like the luckiest martial artist in the world to be here at this time, this place and this moment.

Life does go in circles.

Well, not only did I have sushi with my forms hero JOHN CHUNG but the SIL-LUM Kung-Fu instructor himself GRAND MASTER LEO FONG, A LIVING LEGEND who taught me from his book thirty one years ago.

But you know what was the most exciting part, I mean knock your socks off part, was having my son meet my heroes and to teach him the lesson of making a friend that will last him a lifetime – that was priceless.

BUSHIDO
THE CODE OF THE SAMURAI

Samurai have no reason to be cruel.
They do not need to prove their strength.
A Samurai is courteous even to his enemies.
Without this outward show of respect,
We are nothing more than animals.
A Samurai is not only respected
for his strength in battle,
But also by his dealing with other men.
The true inner strength of a samurai becomes
Apparent during difficult times.

Chapter 3

Black Belt Television

If You Build It

They Will Come

Black Belt Television
If You Build It They Will Come

By Chip Youngblood

Television was invented in the twenties and seventy years later there still was not a full time Martial Arts channel. Although there had been lots of talk there were no results, until recently.

Airwaves Of Martial Arts "Black Belt Television If You Build It, They Will Come"

In November 2004, Black Belt TV was launched into seventeen million homes, giving the Martial Artist a venue to reach everyone with their message. Here is the journey of one man's dream of creating a twenty-four hour, in your face, real Martial Arts channel and giving the sponsors the chance to get on board to showcase their products to the world.

"Black Belt Television If You Build It, They Will Come"

I am sitting on the plane thinking of the past two weeks as being the roller coaster ride of my career. Spending two weeks with Professor Gary Lee is unlike anything I would have ever expected. He is a warrior and sage that has experienced many unexpected adventures.

However let's start from the beginning. It was a year ago when I was asked to cover the Super Grands in Houston, Texas. The Super Grands is a spectacular event, a gathering of superb Black Belts and past Superstars.

I first saw Professor Gary Lee at the Super Grands where he was the master of ceremonies for the finals. He was a figure to behold, wearing his Hakama and Kimonos. He looked as if he were a samurai in the wrong century. I set up a meeting that would change my mind and my attitude towards Martial Arts.

Professor Lee has had an incredible career in the Martial Arts. He is a historian of sport Karate in America, NBL World Champion, and International Competitor for over Thirty Years, Actor, Producer, Black Belt Hall of Famer. Professor Lee regards his career as, "A constant learning process of information for as long as I can remember."

He came from his home land of Hawaii with hardly anything. However, he survived living on the Mainland, with no family or guidance, thanks to his Karate God Fathers, as he calls them.

The Karate men who have been a part of his life since his early teenage years are, Jim Harrison, Dr. Maung Gyi, Mako, Allen Steen, Jerry Piddington, Mike Stone, Sam Chapman, Ted Tabura, John Kuhl (deceased), George Minshew, Carl Geis, Andrew Tamper, George Anderson, Robert Trias (deceased), Sensei Kishi, Sid Campbell (deceased), Glenn Kwan, Ed Parker (deceased) Ed Daniel, Al Gene Carulia, Ernie "Radar" Smith (deceased).

This was an incredible array of present and past legends of the Martial Arts. Tears come to his eyes when he talks about each legends and how each one played an important part in his career. The Living Legend has had the honor of roasting three of his heroes. No wonder Professor Lee is the man and the leader he is today.

When we were done with the interview, Professor Lee said he had a project in the works, but did not know all the details yet. He said, "I will call you in a year. I will have a grasp of the project then and if it hits, it will be the biggest and most exciting contribution to the Martial Arts in a long time. A full time television channel totally dedicated to Martial Arts with educational values and high-class entertainment as a start. It's called 'BLACK BELT TV'."

Much effort has gone into this project of getting a national Martial Arts station up and running, but no one had a personality like Professor Gary Lee or his martial arts contacts.

The Metronome Company who owns BLACK BELT TV and one of the producers, Erik D. Jones, approached Professor Lee. They offered Professor Lee a contract to do a Martial Arts show called "Martial Arts Exclusive" a Martial Arts variety show with fun as it's priority. They would travel around the country filming everything from tournaments, talent contest, expos, and special Karate promotions. Professor Gary Lee has interviewed the following celebrities for Black Belt TV, Eric Lee, Al Dacascos, Sid Campbell, Gene LeBell, Alan Goldberg, Ed Daniel, J. Pat Burleson, Tim Kirby, Cynthia Rothrock, Stephen Hayes, James Lew, Bernie "Pops" Krasnoo, Arnold Urquidez, Blinky Rodriguez, Chung Lee, Don "The Dragon" Wilson, Kathy Long, Bill Ryusaki, Ice T., Keith Weston, Lawrence Arthur, James Hong, Bill Viola, Boice Lydell and many more. The most memorable event of the show was the demonstrations.

Professor Lee is known for his spectacular sword demonstrations, which he perfected during his twenty years of performing at Six Flags Astroworld.

When asked about his sword training Gary smiled and said -

"I wanted to train as close as I could to the samurai, so I modeled my self after great swordsmen like, Toshiro Mifune, Hidy Ochiai, Tadashi Yamashita, Dale Kirby and Sonny Chiba.

These were the master swordsmen who inspired me. I remember watching the Iaido guys go out into the jungle and come back covered in blood, week after week, six to ten guys dressed in Hakama, carrying their sword over their shoulders.

One day I decided to follow them. I kept my distance and crept my way through the thick jungle, sometimes crawling on the ground so I wouldn't be seen or heard. Besides, I was scared to death that I had enough nerve to follow them.

From a distance I saw them work their swords and boken for about an hour, then I saw a group of locals bringing in cages. In the cages were pigs. The locals would tie the legs and grab each end of the huge pig and then throw it at the master swordsman. He then would draw and cut directly in two pieces.

Now I know where the blood came from and later I found out they were doing this for the huge picnics (Luau) for the tourist. All the pigs went to roast in the sandpit."

One particular interview at the Martial Arts History Museum grand opening ceremonies in Burbank, California really surprised me. That interview was between Professor Gary Lee and Grandmaster Hidy Ochiai.

You could tell by their expression and friendship they were old warriors of a past sport gone but not forgotten by these two. I got a little closer so I could hear their conversation and what I heard was them comparing different cuts they have made on human bodies with their katanas.

Professor Lee would say "I have done it with watermelons and cantaloupes" and the Master Ochiai would respond "Gary that is good but have you cut apples on rice paper and not cut the paper?"

Professor Lee would say "Ous" and then say "I have cut seven cucumbers on the throat, neck, stomach and groin" and Master Ochiai would say, "Yes Gary, I have too but I was blindfolded."

Then Professor Lee said, "Sensei my greatest cut was at the World Martial Arts Tournament where I cut a lemon and then a slice of lemon on the neck of my uki."

Master Ochiai laughed and said, "Gary don't you remember at the Battle of Atlanta I cut a rice grain in half on my uki's forehead?" Professor Lee has tears running down his cheek and stood up and bowed and said, "Sir, I am honored, you are samurai, Ous!"

Paramount Movie Studios, a local TV news show and Black Belt TV witnessed a remarkable interview that was rare and very personal.

Well a year went by and I received the phone call from Hawaiirock Productions. Professor Lee had some great news he said, "Black Belt TV will be on the air November 2004."

The word got out quickly and with anything great comes competition. When I asked professor Lee about the competition of another network or even somebody else saying they are Black Belt TV, he laughs and says, "Well I can promise you this, no one has beat the streets harder than I, my crew and my Black Belt TV producers to give the un-biased reporting we do and a little logo in a couple of magazines is not going to change all the hard work and traveling my team has done to get us up and running and on the air."

Professor Lee and I were picked up by a black limo at the airport and driven to the downtown area of Houston. The skyline is beautiful and Houston is a great city. The limo driver dropped me off at a tall building and said for me to go to the top floor and I would be met by another one of Professor Lee's staff.

I did what I was told and when I got to the roof Professor Lee's assistant Susan Thompson met me. The first thing she asked me was, if I was afraid of heights. That was strange. Well she walked over to a round circle and then I saw a helicopter come out of nowhere and land next to us. Then she told me to get in the helicopter and enjoy the ride.

Professor Lee wanted me to see the whole city from a different view. What an experience. When we landed on top of another building an hour later, there he was, Professor Gary Lee. We went down a couple of flights and walked into this huge seafood restaurant and had a great dinner.

The next couple of days I would be out of breath trying to keep up with the professor. When the smoke had settled after his long days in the Martial Arts, we would hang out next to his little two acre bass pond and talk about Black Belt TV and how it is going to change the future of Martial Arts advertising and how we are the pioneers of a new area.

Professor Lee said, "The Martial Arts needs a complete station with unbiased programming, going after all communities and cultures. For example a show for teens, and young adults, a Martial Arts Christian show, Animation Black Belt Style, and All Spanish teaching show with well-known Spanish speaking masters. How about an Eric Lee celebrity show? Remember Michele "The Mouse" Krasnoo, one of the most popular sport Karate players ever? She wants a show too."

If you build it, they will come.

BUSHIDO
THE CODE OF THE SAMURAI

Rise up above the masses of people that are afraid to act.
Hiding like a turtle in a shell is not living at all.
A Samurai must have heroic courage.
It is absolutely risky. It is dangerous.
It is living life completely, fully, wonderfully.
Heroic courage is not blind. It is intelligent and strong.
Replace fear with respect and caution

Chapter 4
The Draw

The Draw

In the sixties, martial art weapons had not been introduced into martial arts events around the country, in fact the half time shows were either weapons demonstrations or self defense techniques displayed because they were spectacular to watch. Sooner or later producers got smart.

The legendary karate Master, Sid Campbell was one of the first to introduce weapons competition on the west coast and the great Master Aaron Banks introduce weapons on the east coast.

One of the Museum of Sport Karate's™ all-time favorite martial arts weapons performers was Hanshi Andrew Linick, who won countless weapon's kata championships.

He would dazzle thousands of spectators with his flawless skill and his rare talent mystified audiences and judges alike. His Okinawan weapons expertise included: Nunchaku, Sai, Bo, Kama, Tonfa and Sword. Grandmaster Linick is known by his peers as the teacher's teacher or the Okinawan Weapon's Technician.

Some of the super stars of weapons in the sixties and seventies were Eric Lee, Al Dacascos, Tadashi Yamashita, Andrew Linick Ph.D, Hidy Ohcai, Dale Kirby, Cindy Rothrock, Mark Dacascos, James Lew, Phillip Koppel, James Cook and many, many others.

In the early seventies weapons had a division of their own and anything was allowed, Kung Fu, Staffs, Sai, all the Kobudo weapons, farm tools and even spears.

At the 1981 Fort Worth Pro-Am, in Fort Worth, Texas, a competitor pulled a 357 Magnum pistol fill with blanks and shot at the judges. It was very loud and frightening. He was arrested, but it shook up the crowd. I hit the floor and dove behind a chair. I took third place that day. It was the loudest third place I had ever won.

To me, the most tenacious of all martial art weapons is the sword and I have studied it with great reverence. I have seen it used both in the past and in the present by many who compete or perform. So often I see it used improperly.

It would make me nervous when I saw someone wearing a sword upside down or touching the blade, or letting some one touch the blade. It hurt to see them drop the blade, or cut himself or the uki. Sometimes the competitor would loose the blade and it would go into the audience and hit some innocent bystander! In those days there were no medics on hand and it was scary stuff.

The draw should be pure, touched by no one except the competitor and the owner of the sword. After you draw you clean your sword, oil your sword and clean your sword again. Why, because a good blade should be nourished, taken care of like a brother, with responsibility. The blade is your partner and you become one, because in a different time, your life depended on it.

I had a spectacular experience competing with the sword in Guatemala City in 1993. There were some 5,000 Guatemalans in the audience and their cheering was deafening.

When I walked on stage and drew the sword, they became utterly silent, I could hear only the thunder, and the bright light of the lighting cracked around me in the huge outside dome. Special super star guest, Bill Ryusaki, said "I have never seen someone awe and quiet a huge crowd like this since Bruce Lee performed at the Long Beach Internationals. It was amazing!

There is always someone at a Sport Karate event if there is a weapons division that draws. You may not see him or know he is there, but if you disrespect his sword he will let you know, yes I said "his sword".

You never see the purest drawers competing at a sport karate event because drawing for them is not display. I do believe in competing with the sword and demonstrating the sword. Kabuki acting at it's finest. Drawing at your best. But I understand those who do not wish to compete or perform in demonstrations, as theirs is a different world.

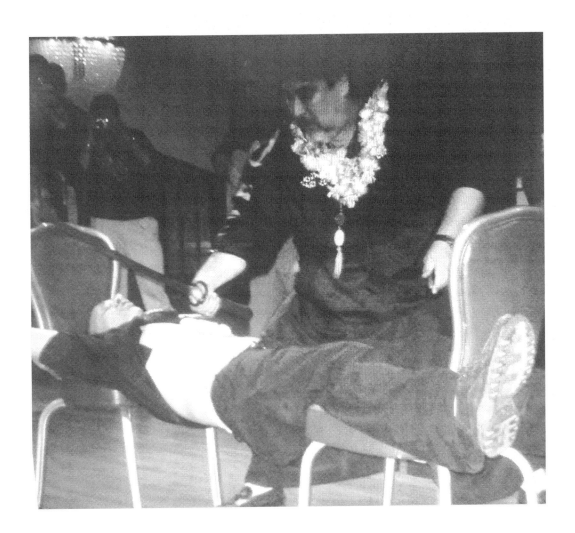

BUSHIDO
THE CODE OF THE SAMURAI

A true Samurai has only one judge of his honor,
And that is himself.
Decisions you make and how these decisions are
carried out are a reflection of who you truly are.
You cannot hide from yourself.

Chapter 5
The Old Japanese Fisherman

The Old Japanese Fisherman

I have many fond memories of martial arts events from my childhood in Hawaii. There are things I will never forget, like watching the Kyokushin-Kai Karate class training in the ocean under the moonlight, practicing kata and Seichan breathing while the waves crash against their bodies. There were easily over fifty Black Belts who practiced with their hard animal attitudes.

I remember secretly following the drawers and cutters of our dojo out in the deep woods and watching as they would draw and cut live pigs for the Lua's and feast of the islands. These men were truly dangerous men, but they were so kind and gentle in their personal ways. Their karate was very strong, and when they put on their Hakama I could see and feel a change.

Twice a week I would make an excuse to Sensei and sneak through my path in the woods to follow these very different kind of warriors. Sensei did not draw, but he allowed this small group of men to work out at the dojo and they had swords!

At first I simply wondered why their trips into the woods left them covered in blood as I watched them washing off down in the ocean. I was caught the very first time I followed them and, of course, I suffered the consequences of a "never do that again" lecture. I didn't listen because the draw was just to compelling. I simply found a better way to follow them.

Do not put your hands in the cookie jar or else!!!

I was a eleven year old kid with adventure as my middle name and my adventures led me to Toshirio. He was a fisherman who made his living throwing nets early in the morning and again in the early evening when the fish came to life again after the heat of the day.

He was very precise with his fishing nets, working the fine loose nylon threads, swaying back and forth, getting the net exactly where he wanted it. Watching him was mesmerizing, but his talents were not limited to fishing. When he was through with his morning fishing routine, and before he was drawn back to his evenings work at the ocean's edge, he would hand make Bokens.

At first when I watched him I thought he was just twiddling a big stick, but he was actually carving the piece of wood. As I continued to watch I discovered that he was an artist and I wanted to hang out with him when ever I could, even into my ladder years on the Island.

I talked with the students that purchased his gifts and little by little I became a friend of the Boken Master, the name the islanders gave him. I simply called him Toshiro.

The first time Toshiro invited me to his house, I saw so many sticks in his yard. I wondered why? I soon learned! He would work on white pine or red oak or driftwood from the sea, ah, but before he would do the first knife cut on any piece of wood, he would place it in his yard and watch it for a week. He believed he could feel the spirit of each piece of wood he worked on.

I shared about my new friend with Sensei Kishi and he thought the relationship would be a good experience for me. I remembered he laugh when I told him how I had met him. Sensei said, "Normally he scares anyone to heck and back when they get caught watching him, lucky for you he liked you!"

In the summers of 1966, 67, 68 and 69 I learned his craft of making a Boken. A Boken is the symbol of a live sword, but made of wood. It is extremely hard, depending on the wood chosen, and it must be hand sanded and carved into a weapon with skill and accurateness. The Handle had to be gripped tightly by the warrior and some even wrapped the handle.

Toshiro never wrapped, and was against it. He felt it took away from the purity of the weapon. The goal was to form a blade of wood that was dangerous and practical for practice or a duel, and it must have a very practical point.

The night before my Black Belt test, Toshiro invited me over to his little hut and gave me my first Boken. It was White Pine and battered from practicing against a live sword. I could feel the battles this Boken had experienced. Toshiro handed me a pineapple and said "Gary-san, hold it up here, pointing at my chest, and don't breathe!" He then speared the pineapple through with a thrusting motion, smooth, accurate and deadly, stopping just at my skin! Without emotion, he pulled the wooden sword out of the pineapple, cleaned it and said "This piece of wood has saved my life more than once".

As he gave the Boken back to me, he told me that the hard scale on the outside of the pineapple is important to pierce first, the meat of the pineapple symbolizes the bones and odd stuff inside the body, but the important part is to stop before you penetrate the holder.

I could not take my cherished Boken on the plane with me to the Mainland, so I gave it to Sensei Kishi and he cherished it until his death, and yes, I put it in his coffin when I came back to the Islands to bury him. I looked for Toshiro when I was back, but rumors were he had returned to Japan, to his little fishing village, to retire near his family and friends. Whenever I see a Boken in stores and all the dojo's I have visited I think of Toshiro and his knife carving away.

BUSHIDO
THE CODE OF THE SAMURAI

Through intense training,
The Samurai becomes quick and strong.
He is not as other men.
He develops a power that must be used
for the good of all.
He has compassion.
He helps his fellow men at every opportunity.
If an opportunity does not arise,
He goes out of his way to find one.

Chapter 6

Hawaiian Son

Texas Star

Hawaiian Son – Texas Star

By Duane R. Ethington

Think about it for a moment. Before you are even six years old you lose your parents in a tragic airplane accident. You have only one relative, an uncle you don't even know who turns out to be cruel towards you. You have no family, no friends, and a bleak outlook on what might seem like no life at all, with no foreseeable future.

What do you do?

Many, many folks would give up or easily fall into the wrong crowds and spend the rest of their lives getting into trouble. Basically, they would give up on life before they even had a chance to live it.

But GARY LEE certainly is not your average person. Young Gary took this pot of despair, loneliness and heartbreaking travesty and turned it into a banquet of life. Not only has Gary Lee pulled himself from nothing to an enviable career in the martial arts and life, but he has done it with a style and grace that can only be the envy of most people around him.

How this remarkable man achieved a life so full and rich from such a desolate beginning is a phenomenal story in itself.

Many avenues could have been taken by the young boy. With an uncle who yelled at him a lot, a house with no TV or radio or air conditioning and a life that wasn't much fun for a six year old, it could have gone bad.

But Gary thanks God every day for that walk on the beach the day he topped the little sand dune and made the discovery that would literally change his life.

Following the strange grunting sounds, young Gary discovered himself before a small hut where he found a hole big enough to look through. There he saw a small group of Kenpo black belts training under the watchful eye of a stern-faced sensei. The six year old had never seen anything like it and was 'hooked' immediately.

"I'd sneak out at night to watch them." laments Gary. "Even though I knew I would get yelled at and probably hit or punished in some other way."

From that very first look at the black belts Gary knew that this was what he wanted to be involved in for the rest of his life. He had no way of knowing that martial arts would not only consume his own life but change many lives which would cross his path in later years.

The stern-faced sensei turned out to be Sensei Kishi.

To this day, Gary does not understand how it came about as his uncle would not even disclose it on his deathbed, but Sensei Kishi came over one day and told the young boy that from now on he would be living with him.

"I think my uncle traded me for something." says Gary of the incident now so far in his past.

However it came about, the fact that young Gary, now seven years old, was placed with Sensei Kishi was probably the best thing that could have ever happened to him.

For seven days a week, every day, for the next seven years, Gary Lee ate, breathed and lived martial arts. This way of life was implanted into the core of his very being.

The road wasn't easy by any means. A young boy training with a bunch of seasoned black belts brought plenty of bruises and lumps as well as an acquisition of a vast amount of knowledge which would stick with Gary for the rest of his life.

This phase of the young Hawaiian's life would not be complete without the retelling of 'The Tale of the Forty Brooms'.

If you want a first hand version, hang out with Gary Lee and ask him. For this abbreviated version, I will put it in Gary's own words so you might understand the significance of the lesson learned.

"Once, and only once, did I ever raise my voice or smart off to Sensei." says Gary with a raised eyebrow as he, undoubtedly, remembers every moment of the event. "I wanted to go surfing as the waves were breaking some ten to fifteen feet off the north shore. Sensei said "No". A bad storm was brewing. Impatiently, I told him that all I ever did was train and I wanted to go surfing. No surfing today, was Sensei's short response. But I want to go surfing, was my only answer."

At this point, Gary just shakes his head as he recalls the unfolding of the day back then.

"I had never seen Sensei look at me the way he did that day." continues Gary. "Instead of surfing, I was instructed to go to town and bring back some brooms that Sensei had ordered. The store, by the way, was about ten miles away.

Why would sensei send a nine year old boy so far on foot to get brooms? I remember how mad I was and I cried most of the way there and back. It rained a cold, hard rain almost all the way of my journey into town.

Later I heard that two surfers had drowned in the pounding waves. Suddenly, it hit me. Sensei knew the danger and was only protecting me, as always, when he refused to let me go. I had only been thinking of myself and probably would have gotten killed had I gone.

The lesson learned was this - I should never question Sensei. He is Sensei, the teacher, and he deserves all the respect I can give him.

Just do it and do it without an attitude. Never talk back and respect your peers and most importantly, never question Sensei. Respect! Respect! Respect! Ous.

What happened with the brooms, you might ask?

That night, in class, Sensei demonstrated Kyoshi-jujitsu. After giving each student a broom, he instructed them to attack him as they wished.

One by one, with flawless technique, Sensei would break the attacking brooms, which represented arms, with a precise blow. He would break low for a wrist, medium for an elbow or high for a forearm. To this day, I have never witnessed anything like it again.

Sensei stopped at 39 brooms and handed me the last broom. With over 30 black belts watching, he had me strike at him. He caught the handle of the broom and swept me to the floor and then swept my face and body, all in about 3 or 4 seconds.

Then he gave me the unbroken broom and told me that he wanted me to sweep the front of the dojo (which was sand) every day until I left. Without question or hesitation I said yes and swept the front of that dojo every day for the next five years. Then I left for the mainland after I got my black belt at age 14."

Even getting that black belt was not easy for Gary. Sensei Kishi failed Gary on his first test try, saying that he didn't have the proper attitude. Six months later, Gary passed with flying colors.

When he left Hawaii in 1969, it was with a small backpack, his black belt, a copy of the 1968 Black Belt Yearbook, a cream colored Gordon and Smith Surf Board and that broom.

Family

With the passing of his only living relative, the uncle, Gary Lee was truly all alone in a huge world.

However, the kid with the big heart and huge smile and a vast thirst for knowledge and adventure soon found himself welcome in many martial arts circles. Gary Lee adopted the martial arts community as his new family. People like Ed Parker, Mike Stone, Sid Campbell, Masayuki Ward, Mako and Jack Farr became his 'fathers figures'. Others who Gary learned from and learned great respect for were Jim Harrison, Sam Chapman Steve Fisher, Sensei Nakumara, Joe Corley, Dan Anderson , John Townsley, Andrew Tamper along with countless others.

Now a proud father of Garett and a devoted and loving husband to Tammy, his wife of 26 years, Gary has a solid anchor in his life and a family that he can be very proud of. "Tammy came in as a 'try-out' student one day and has never left." says Gary with a huge smile. "She is my rock."

The Journey

Gary Lee's martial arts accomplishments could fill a book and are far too numerous to reveal in a story like this. However, to give you a small idea of the tremendous impact Mr. Lee has had on the martial arts world I will list but a very few of his accomplishments.

Gary Lee has placed in EVERY tournament he has entered for THIRTY years. He is the only competitor to win two tournaments in the SAME DAY. The Dragon Rock AOK Open and The National Black Belt League Masters, fighting. Kata, weapons.

For years he gave daily martial arts shows and demonstrations at Houston's Astroworld and Six Flags where he performed over 5,000 shows. 1982-90

Texas State B.A.S.S. Federation Champion 1987 National Weapons Champion USAKF, Gold Medalists 1992. He has been ranked in the TOP TEN for A.O.K., NBL, SOCK, SKI, USAKF, TNT Lead actor for The Hollywood Stunt Show and Comedy Hour, Six Flags 1993-94.

He is the creator of The Living Legends Celebrity Roast. Gary Lee has been inducted into several Black Belt Hall of Fames and has garnered countless plaques and awards for 'Outstanding Contributions to the Martial Arts'. He has won the Golden Greek Award., Texas MVP 1997 He was one of the feature actors in Sidekicks, The Movie. He has choreographed multi-movie stunt scenes.

Gary Lee has excelled outside the martial arts world, as well, in winning the Texas State B.A.S.S Fishing Championship and spends his time giving countless seminars to youngsters and adults on the finer points of bass fishing at the Houston and Dallas Boat Shows since 1987.

He is sponsored as a Pro-Staff for Denver Marine, N .C, Ranger Boats, Lone Star Graphite Rods, Greg Bingam's Check- It – Stick and "The Dock Buster" Flippen Stick Flow-Rite of Tennessee, Fish Formula, Worden Lures and He still fishes all the major tournaments in Texas and surrounding states.

Another of Gary Lee's passionate dreams is coming into fruition. That is the construction and opening of The Sport Martial Arts Museum.

Gary said "The Museum Of Sport Karate will be the last event that I will work on. I have collected the finest minds in the world as History Generals to help do the documentation and history analysis of our sport and when we are though it will be a fun, entertaining, educational and informative site for the family or the hard level traditionalist."

When asked to pick one out of his many stories and and his absolute favorite he was very quiet for a moment, looked up at the camera and said " I do have one that is always with me and it happened along time ago."

"I remember working out in Ohio and visiting many, many studios. This one dojo was so intimidating I would cry and get myself all in a mess before I walked in. One day, I was two doors down from the studio and getting ready, when I heard a voice. It said "Hey kid why are you crying? It is just Karate."

The man's name was Al Hippert; he was just coming back from his third tour of Vietnam, where he was covert operator and a tunnel rat. He was a real serious person.

He had been training at the dojo I was at, but I never seen him before. He was small but stocky and he had the look. That Stare! It was almost creepy. Heck, it was creepy!!

He asked me to work out with him and it change my life. He was first a Karate man and then JUDO consumed his life.

When he first asked me to Randori, I assumed it was sparring, punching, kicking all that stuff. It turned out to be choking, joint locking, passing out, finger manipulation, arm barring and of course roto-segin nagi and ippon segin nagi, thousands of times, throws, take downs, sweeps, stomps, elbow strikes and of course head butts.

And anything goes until you tapped out or you were choked out, he taught me how to fight for real, life and death situations, mentally to be prepared and have PMA.

He also taught me about life, the manners, the yes sirs and the no sirs, to help a needful person and to help that one kid who has to mentally get in tune with himself before the pressure of life.

That is the story that stays with me the most for he was one of the first mainland sensei's to touch my life and give me direction to where I was going.

He hurt me to teach me! I think about him everyday, every moment whenever I feel pain!

I have been in the martial arts for nearly forty years, myself, and can tell you from the heart that Gary Lee is on a small list I have of those whom I truly respect above all others. He is a Texas transplanted Hawaiian with a tremendous heart and a man I am proud to call friend.

From a Hawaiian boy lost on the beach, Gary Lee has grown to be a force in the martial arts world and a leader in life. He is truly a Hawaiian Son who has become a Texas Star and he deserves our respect. OUS!

BUSHIDO
THE CODE OF THE SAMURAI

When a Samurai has said he will perform an action,
It is as good as done.
Nothing will stop him from completing
what he has said he will do.
He does not have to "give his word".
He does not have to "promise".
The action of speaking alone
has set the act of doing in motion.
Speaking and doing are the same action.

Chapter 7
Thoughts From The Japanese Waterman

Thoughts From The Japanese Waterman

Hitch Hiking Across America - A Day To Remember!

I was nineteen years old, hitchhiking for the third time across the United States chasing waves with my little five - seven Gordon twin fin surfboard right outside Oklahoma City, Oklahoma.

I stopped in a little convenient store for a soda pop and was in back of the store when I heard in a loud voice "Give the money or I will shoot you, I mean it, I will shoot you and your Dog!

For some reason I thought of my little dog I had in Hawaii and I didn't care about the gun, foolish but instinct set in. I grabbed a couple of can goods and a shovel I saw, threw the cans to the right and hit him on the left in the head with the shovel, the robber fell dropping his gun.

The store owner kicked the gun away and soon the police arrived. The store owner made me out to be a hero but in my heart I was saving the dog and I just acted out of instinct to survive, it was my first encounter with a gun since I had come to the mainland and my Sword training had given me ability's, even with a shovel.

The store owner offered me money for what I did but I could not take money for something I would have done anyway, naturally.

Now that I am much older I realize how I reacted back then wasn't the smartest thing to do and in my mind I have analyzed what I did and still believe it was thinking of him shooting that little dog, not the owner and it did not even occur to me at the moment I could have been shot or been killed. All I cared about was him saying he was going to shoot an animal.

Martial arts teaches you not to think but react at the moment the occasion arrives. The thinking should be done in the Dojo or Kwoon where you have your teacher to help you and teach you to make the right decisions. However reality is a different animal.

I can remember distinctly, I did not think about the future or the fact of danger, just I did not want a little dog to be shot and that is when courage took over.

The training of martial arts teaches you to be smart, that is why I threw the cans to make assailant look the other way, the shovel was the weapon at hand and I thought of all those times I saw Kyoshi hit his students with his Shinai and whacked them across the head just for not paying attention or just his personal punishment he would give us because that is the way they did the training back in the day or at least in Hawaii.

Why did I pick up the shovel instead of using my Karate?

Well I was taught in my weapons training that the weapon that you train with, any weapon was a extension of my hands, there fore, I did think of Karate even though I hit him in the head with the shovel, mind you, all this happened in a few seconds - a flash before my eyes. If it wasn't for Karate and for the intense training I did in Hawaii, it might have turned out different.

Thank goodness I didn't have to hit him with my surfboard, it's funny though that afternoon right out of Oklahoma City, it is super flat desert land and it was the first time I saw the Black clouds of a major storm. It got real quiet and from the sky huge pieces of ice started falling hard. It was the first time I encountered a Hailstorm.

I put my Gordon and Smith Twin-fin surfboard, my pride and joy, next to my Tonfas I carried. I put the surfboard over my head to protect me . My hands were beat to bleeding and after the hail storm my board was battered up with huge holes in it .

I remember digging a hole in the desert and burying the surfboard and crying not wanting to leave it in the desert.

What a day! I almost got shot, hit a guy with a shovel, saved a little dog, experience my first hail storm, buried my best friend - the surfboard and was heading toward another karate event.

I love Karate !

Yu

{Heroic Courage} *Rise up above the masses of people that are afraid to act.*

Hiding like a turtle in a shell is not living at all.

A samurai must have heroic courage.

It is absolutely risky. It is dangerous.

It is living life

completely, fully, wonderfully.

Heroic courage is not blind. It is intelligent and strong.

Replace fear with respect and Caution.

BUSHIDO
THE CODE OF THE SAMURAI

For the Samurai, having done some "thing"
Or said some "thing",
He knows he owns that "thing".
He is responsible for it
And all the consequences that follow.
A Samurai is immensely loyal to those in his care.
To those he is responsible for, he remains fiercely true.

Chapter 8
Four Fingers Of Death

Four Fingers Of Death

There are so many Texas legends that have influenced my career here in Texas since I blew in from Hawaii in 1979 but one of the most colorful personalities has to be D.P.Hill from Dallas. D.P was a great Champion and friend.

He was the first brother to become a Black Belt under the Allen Steen list of Legends in a time it was not easy to become a Black Belt. This is one of my favorite memories, not the bloody nose but the friendship I developed with one of the great legends of Texas sport Karate, Master D.P Hill.

The Great D.P Hill "Four Fingers Of Death", a Texas Legend, a great man and friend, he is missed but will never be forgotten!

A flash back....

1981

I am at Tim Kirby's Sunbelt open and fighting "Outrageous" Jerry Jones one of D.P Hill's Black Belt. He was about 6'2 and as you know I am about 5'7, D.P, Ant Allen, Calvin Cross, Chuck Timmons and the Dallas entourage was cheering him on.

D.P did not know me but he used to love to watch my Kata and he noticed I had no coach or anyone cheering for me. So, he walked to my side of the ring and in his gruff unique way of talking said –

"I like Gary Lee. If no body going to coach Gary Lee, i'm going to coach Gary Lee. You don't mind me coaching you Gary Lee? I'd like you kata, I'd help you beat my student Gary Lee. You'd just got to listen to me. I'd just

show you how to beat 'outragous". He don't listen to me anyway. Punch him Gary Lee. Punch him "

I was kind of freaking out but I thought it was so cool of him doing what he did. Of course, "Outrageous" hit me with that patented jump spin back kick and busted my nose.

Blood everywhere!

Grand Master James Toney was the center, he gave me some paper towels and said "Welcome to Texas".

D.P came up to me and said "You need to learn the art of ducking".

We became such good friends. Every time I would see him after that I always showed my love and respect and of we got to Roast him with a Celebrity Roast.

A great memory, Master D.P Hill!

Rest in Peace.

Chapter 9

What Does Not Kill You Makes You Stronger

What Does Not Kill You Makes You Stronger
By Jim Butin

Back in the day, actually in 1967 when I was 17 and ready to test for 1st Brown, Allen Steen was hosting a test in Dallas. I was a Ft. Worth boy under Pat Burleson, and thought that Karate in Texas was one big family.

So I drove to Dallas and threw my money down to test. Mr. Steen asked me, "Does Mr. Burleson know that you are here?". I was puzzled but probably replied, "I think so!"

Obviously this was a situation that probably had not occurred before, but Mr. Steen called Mr. Burleson and the test soon began. Keith Yates was testing for 4th or 3rd Brown and Roy Kurban was testing for 2nd Brown that day, and we all passed the exam.

About 6 months later Mr. Burleson told me that it was time for me to test for Black Belt. I really was caught off guard, I had never won a trophy in competition until I had made Brown Belt and I had won six in a row including a victory over Pat Worley for 1st place in Austin, so I was enjoying success and was not sure I wanted to dance with the big boys yet.

I had watched a Black Belt test with three of the toughest guys in our organization. I saw Chuck Loven, Ron Moffitt, and David Melville all take a tough exam and all pass.

What I did not notice (until I became wiser) was that at most only two candidates at a time were sparring as our studio was small on Camp Bowie and one was resting. When my exam was held it was 101 degrees on June 8,

1968, the floor was pie shaped and the one window unit air conditioner was blowing on the exam table.

There were no other candidates for Black belt and I had a group of superstars waiting in line to hurt me if they could. Bill Watson, John and Pat Worley, Larry Carnahan, and others my blurred memory can't recall were in attendance.

I don't know how many fights I had, but I do remember sitting on the floor, and trying to get up to say, "I have to stop, I can't do anymore!". When someone picked me up, Mr. Burleson said, "You, and you ...Get him!" Fortunately that was the last match (or there may have been a recorded death!). Later I wondered if my trip to Dallas for testing, had a little "Pay back" attached to it that I never considered.

Oh well, what does not kill you, makes you stronger!

Grand Master Jim Butin
Original History General
Museum Of Sport Karate

Chapter 10
The Apple Does Not Fall Far From The Tree

The Apple Does Not Fall Far From The Tree

This next story is a little close to the heart. It is the amazing Karate journey my son has taken. The story is still changing every day. He is a warrior and dedicated to Texas Sport Karate and it's rich tradition of fighting spirit and creating national Champions.

It all started with an incredible Black Belt test in front of a group of legends in the sport and winning the US Open and Battle of Atlanta in the same year.

Garett was at the right place at the right time and he will never forget what it is to be Born A Texas Karate Warrior.

Garett Robert Lee was born in Houston, Texas on January 10th 1992 into a family of Martial Artist. His father is well known across America as an excellent competitor, knowledgeable Black Belt and founder of the Living Legends Celebrity Roast. Garett's mother holds a Black Belt and she was a winning competitor during her competition years as an under belt and Brown Belt.

Long time friend and World Full- Contact Karate Champion Ishmael Robles said at Garett's Black Belt Test, *"Garett is destined to be the next layer of champions Texas produces, but the main reason he is going to be a champion is because he was born in Texas!"*

Garett has been immersed in martial arts since his father hung toy throwing stars and nunchaku above Garett's crib. He was competing by the age of two and performing on stage with his father across America.

Rumor has it that his dad would drop him off at karate schools and leave for hours, some time for days. It is a fact that he would leave him at the SHAOLIN TEMPLES around Houston so he could learn Kung Fu with the live-in Monks.

He fought his first full-contact kickboxing match at age six at Rumble At Roundrock World Championships. He won fifty first places in forms and fighting from National Blackbelt League, Texas Tour, A.O.K, Texas Karate Organization and Sport Karate International...wait a minute, kids can't really be Black Belts, they have no power and they can't do all the things a real Black Belt does.

WHAT IS A REAL BLACK BELT?

Garett earned his black belt at seven years of age. That was unheard of in the real karate world and thought to be of a farce. No child was seen as capable of breaking boards, fighting, self-discipline, attitude, bunkai, kobudo weapons, and do, ku san ku, jion, ni shi sho ho, unsu, sesien, sanchin sapei (these are all Black Belt Katas), all the wazas, and of course the basic kion katas that are required in Okinawan Karate.

He also endured the pressure of a panel of thirty living legends in the martial arts who graded him. This had never been done before, but that is what makes Garett very special. They passed him and signed his certificate endorsing his skills as a Black Belt.

The reason Garett has excelled in the martial arts and has done almost impossible feats in traditional and sport karate is the fact that he has many teachers!

Garett has performed in many places and in front of thousands of karate spectators but his most cherished memory is when he did his routine at a Celebrity Roast in front of Chuck Norris, Roy D. Kurban, Richard Norton,

Jeff Smith, Troy Dorsey, Steve Fisher, and the great Lou Casamassa.

Grand Master Casamassa had given Garett's dad the sword he used in the demonstration that night. It gave Garett goose bumps because he knew how much his dad loved and respected Grand Master Casamassa. Receiving a sword is the ultimate gift.

Another memorable event was performing on the Super Grands stage at two years of age and breaking a board over his father's head. When he was four years old Bernie "Pops Kransnoo" put him on the Sherman Oaks Raiders National Karate Team and his sport karate career begin. He would perform wherever his father would have a performance.

It was like "Have Blackbelt Will Travel".

Garett has had an incredible traveling career but because he pursued many goals in 2005 we are sharing about that year.

He Who Travels Sees The Water Fall Differently Than Others Who Don't

There Are No Limits To Reaching Our Goals With A PMA (Positive Mental Attitude)

In 2005, Garett started out chasing the A.O.K, the Texas karate circuit. He finish with a number one seed in the east and went in to the State Championship with eight first places in a row in kata and fighting.

After a tremendous year in this circuit, and being picked as the youngest member on Team Focus, he won two state titles; one in 12-13 Black Belt Kata and the other 12-13 Black Belt Fighting.

Then he went to Columbus Ohio for Arnold's Martial Arts Festival as the special guest performer for Black Belt Television.

The legendary Tokey Hill sponsored Garett at the World Karate Federation event, at the festival, where he won kata and fighting.

Sometimes, opportunity comes once in a lifetime and if you don't take advantage of it, it may never come again. This is what Garett experienced in Houston one Saturday.

Stan Witz, a producer from Las Vegas introduced his event in Houston at the Fonde Recreation Center. Ms. Linda Denley was his sponsor and Garett entered all divisions winning everything including the Adult Black Belt Kata division. Then it was on to The Battle of H-town, across Houston to the north side of town, where he won Kata and fighting.

Garett had won two major karate events in one day!

Then he was on his way to Pittsburgh to the National Black Belt League qualifying event for Super Grands in Buffalo New York. He competed in Japanese Kata in a field of thirty competitors. He finished third, securing him a seed at the World Games at the end of the year.

He was on stage as guest performer for ESPN 2, where he performed spectacular feats with Young Song Lee and Dr.Patrick Price. Garett came back home to Victoria, Texas and competed in the NBL Conference Event, where he won both his divisions in kata and fighting, giving him his fighting seed at Super Grands. Event after event he would go to trying to perform better each time, for he was born into show business because of his dad , he was also very talented with a gift old school karate .

One of Garett's favorite events is Wayne Nyugen's TKO'S Ocean State Nationals in Galveston, Texas. Wayne, better known as the "White Ninja" from the movie "Sidekicks", has watched Garett grow up and sponsors him every year at his event.

This year Garett won his fighting division and Kata division and he won his very first Grand Championship. It was very special when Master Nyugen gave Garett a samurai sword for winning his event. In the old days the ultimate gift was getting a sword from your teacher. Then the next event would be one of his biggest yet!

The Black Belt Magazine Reunion and Festival was a huge event in Hollywood, California. All the stars came out for this one and Garett was right in the middle of the action. He was there to audition for a part in the new show "Are You the Next Martial Arts Superstar?"

And he performed on stage for Black Belt Magazine.

He did get to hang out with Gene LeBell, Chris Casamassa, Michele "The Mouse" Krasnoo, John Chung, Eric Lee, Dan "The Beast" Severn, Young Song Lee, World Karate Champion Linda Denley, Leo Fong, George Alexander.

Master Alexander was so impressed with Garett's skills that he asked him to be his Uki for his performance on stage, what an honor!

While he was there he got to work out with some great martial artist like STUART SCHUMANN AND KEN FIRESTONE. Garett is a season traveler and has done more in the past few years in his karate than most people have done in a lifetime.

Now lets go back to 1999 at the Southwest Hilton on a Friday afternoon with a room full of Legends of sport karate, men like Allen Steen, Matsibushi Ward, James Toney, Ishmael Robles, Jim Butin, Jim Harrison and many more testing a young man of seven years old, a three hour exam of a history making event, a Black Belt Test all will remember and tell stories about the Black Belt Test of Garett Lee.

THE TEST AND FOUR HOURS LATER

Garett's Black Belt exam was "an old fashioned BLACKBELT test (meaning something most adults would fail) under Allen Steen, Ed Daniel, Skipper Mullins, Fred Wren, Jim Toney, Jim Butin, Al Garza, Dan Anderson, Royce Young, Linda Denley, Zulfi Ahmed, Jim Harrison, Jimmy "Gato" Tabares, Ishmael Robles, Stacy and Pablo Mejia, Tim Kirby, George Minshew, Glen

Wilson, Larry Ritchie, Richard Jenkins, Ronnie Al, Daryl Stewart Matubushi Ward, Head Of The Okinawan-Japanese Karate Federation, (just to name a few).

Garett performed his basic and advanced techniques, then several weapons kata, then went through his ten forms, fought ten rounds (not including the multiple attacker rounds).

When the dust had settled all the above named Black Belts signed Garett's Black Belt rank certificate and at age seven Garett was the youngest child and very first child Allen Steen And Jim Harrison ever put their signature on. That made history!

His favorite fighters are Tim Kirby, Linda Denley, Wade Kirkpatrick and of course Demetrius ("the Golden Greek") Havanas, and his dad. His favorite forms are Tetsu, Ni Ji Shi Ho, Eagle and Usu.

His Godfather Dr. Maung Gyi, Founder Of Bando Said "He is a worker and future champion of the world, a real champion not a paper tiger. He is a Kata machine and fights like the old days, hard and fast!"

Here is a part of Garett's history that is pure Texas Karate, old school at a young age!

Having been brought up in Texas, Garett has heard all the "war stories" about the great Texans - Demitrius Havanas and other Texas Legends.

His dad took Garett to a tournament in the Austin area when he was in the peewee divisions and they spent the night with fellow Texan Black Belt Tim Kirby.

Garett fell asleep to the stories of Havanas for a lullaby. After being asleep several hours, Garett rose silently, Tim and Garett's dad watched in quiet surprise as Garett performed "Sleep Kata", he then went through a few sparring combinations and then fell back into bed breathing deeply again in a heavy sleep.

The next day as the tournament got under way, Mr. Kirby gave Garett a patch, not just any patch, this patch read "The Golden Greek". This was given to Tim Kirby (from the A.O.K) for being the best all around male Black Belt in Texas in 1981 the year Demetrius Havanas died in a tragic plane crash.

Tim had carried the patch all these years when he would fight out of state and it was priceless to him, but Garett had touched his heart and Tim was compelled to give him the famous patch.

His dad won two Golden Greek Awards in 1997, so Garett knew how important this was even at his early age. Tim told Garett that morning, "I carried this patch everywhere I fought after Greek died and I felt his spirit with me every match, I want you to have it and remember Greek is with you".

Garett makes sure this is on his uniform when he enters the ring.

He does have a life outside of karate. His mom makes sure of that. Garett maintains an A average in school and enjoys playing "video games" of all sorts.

He enjoys fishing; another activity Garett and his father spend time doing together. Garett looks forward to competition but admits its not all about trophies, he enjoys sparring and the "challenge" it brings.

Garett's favorite technique is the Texas chamber sidekick and the ridge hand. Garett says "The side kick I love because I can stop anyone with it and the ridge hand because of its history! J. Pat Burleson and Mike Stone invented the ridge hand but it was Jeff Smith, Linda Denley, Steve Fisher and Garett's dad who perfected it for sport competition"

Garett has three main sponsors - Century Fitness, Team PKKA and of course Hawaiirock Productions. He has had offers from Kellogs of Battle Creek, Ford, Infiniti and Fox TV but his family wants him to concentrate on his education first and his youth next.

Garett has never forgotten the famous last words at his test by Grand Master

Allen Steen, "Your education is your most important journey without it you will not have the vision to carry out the opportunities that await you in the future."

In Kata he runs Sepai and in fighting he has been picked up by World Champion Jason Holmes (JDog) and the PKKA National Karate Team.

He has won every tournament he has entered 3rd place or higher except for SUPER GRANDS in 2008, for the past two years. Pretty impressive because he fights everywhere, any group, any rules. NBL, AOK, TNT, SKI, WKA, PKC, USKA - International rules, Texas rules.

He has won two Texas State Titles in fighting and one in Kata. Just recently he won and placed in The Back Alley Bash, a fight club in Houston, Texas.

To let you know how much intensity this young Texas Warrior has toward sport karate, even now after ten years of living off the road with his father and doing show after show, in town after town, he still loves sport karate!!!

In 2008 at the Masters Hall of Fame he was asked to perform his flawless Japanese Kata "Sepai " in front of the Living Legends of the martial arts and help open the history making event.

Now in 2011, Garett is nineteen years old and is still loving it, with Six major wins in a row for 2011, he is a threat in any tournament he enters and feels strong about his ability to fight the top fighters in the game.

Garett has entered the men heavy weight division and won enough now to realized, he is known as a short heavyweight that is extremely fast and unpredictable and is a clutch player and a comeback from behind genius!

Ask what the future is for Garett and he says "traveling, meeting new friends and seeing old ones but if I had to say one thing to someone, **'Look Good, Fight Good'**".

So, you see the Apple does not fall far from the tree.

Garett Lee earned his Nidan in Shorin-Ryu Japanese Karate, which was presented by his Bushiban Family and Godfathers Dr. Maung Gyi and Matshibushi Ward (Mabo).

It had been over ten years since Garett Lee's last black belt test in front of a legendary board, at seven years old. It all seems surreal, but after ten years of in your face fighting and kata, wins at The Battle of Atlanta, five Texas State titles, and PKC and AOK number one fighting seed and U S Open and U S Championships, Garett had the opportunity to prove his abilities and love for true Karate Do.

Garett, welcome to the Men's Black Belt Division in Karate! Your Junior Years are behind you and now it is time for new beginnings. We are all proud of you.

Happy 18th Birthday from your Dad!

Chapter 11
A Tale Of Two Sports

A Tale Of Two Sports

Bass Fishing Tournament – Karate Style

One of my first public autograph appearances was at Astroworld, Houston Texas. I was sort of out of place. I really did not belong here but Astroworld's media department made me come.

I was surrounded by some of the greatest Basketball and Baseball players in the world. I kept thinking - Why am I here?

It was a great year (1989) and I had brought a couple of winners, signed a new contract with six flags, rated in four different karate groups national and state, created Kids Expo and Hawaiirock Productions and the biggest thrill - winning the B.A.S.S Federation State Championship and represent Texas in the Central Championship.

People have asked me how I could do both and be a Champion at both sports.

I always have the same answer - "IT IS KARATE, MY WAY OF LIFE. KIME! FOCUS AND CATCH BIG FISH!"

This is where my life would change forever and I would be chasing BIG green fish for the rest of my life !

I am a Bass fisherman!

Twenty years of teaching Kids to fish and have fun !!

Are you addicted to Bass fishing?

Do you stop at every Tackle shop you see even if it's going the other way on the freeway to check out just if they have a new spinning Lure?

Are you so bad that you start thinking about your next trip as soon as you get out of the water to hook your boat from the trip you just did?

It is Friday night and you pull into the motel. The parking lot is full of boats all players are getting ready for the next day's event.

You notice that most the guys and pros are at the local guide roost talking smack and drinking that legal stuff but you stay at the motel sharpening your lures and fine tuning everything, because you know it is 60% luck and 40% technique.

You have to be prepared for anything that can happen and Murphy's law always kicks in when you do not expect it.

Finally, you go to bed.

You close your eyes and count BIG Bass in the live well.

ALARM!!!!!!!!!!!!

It is 3:00 am.

Grab a cup of coffee.

Unplug the Battery charger, secure everything and go to the ramp. Except this event you may ramp anywhere you want, just be at the weigh in at 3:00 pm or be penalized.

You decide to chance it and lose a couple of hour's fish time. But, it will be worth it if your hunch is right.

So, you drive to the other side of the dam to the east for more shade and for the past three days of pre fish you have been following the birds.

The birds find shad, the shad draw fish!!

Sometimes schools of fish form, the shad gather. Sometimes, they will corner thousands of those tiny morsels in a cove or against a set of rocks !

The Pattern !

Black and Blue Stanley Jig with a No.11 black pork frog dipped in Fish Formula and thrown against rocks or structure.

Count to five slow.

Pop or moved slow .

Count to ten this time.

Wait!

The BIG fish!!!

Found a back water cove off the main channel of the river though a maze of Cypress trees.

It was so confusing, you had to spray paint the bottom of the trees to find your way out.

Everything looks fishy.

Which tree??

Then you see an opening.

The first thought was - "Thank you Lord for letting me leaving that spray paint in the boat!"

Then your pre - vision sets in and you see a ripple over by a hanging log.

Another boil.

The buzz bait hooks in the tree for a couple of seconds and falls. Your reel ratio is high speed and you do not make a full turn when he swallows the buzz bait whole.

You do what you have been taught.

Wait three seconds.

You try to break your arm and set the hook !

You know it is a big fish by the way it pulls and the Kistler Rod was the reason you landed the fish .

Two times it went under the Ranger Commache 464 - an old Ranger but it's family.

You believe the worst is going to happen. Lose the fish. Break the rod.

And of course my Kistler came though this time to maybe win my first Championship.

Final weight on BIG fish 9.70

Watch the birds!

You know BIG fish become BIG fish because they feed under the remains of what the schools miss.

A theory.

But it is a pattern and as a Champion you must have many patterns to fish and win; part of that 40% technique you must have.

The Pattern works!

Five fish! One BIG one over nine pounds.

You have culled six times, nineteen bites for eight hours of fishing, really only four hours because of traveling time going to the other ramp!!

You pull up to the weigh in.

They have already had two waves of fisherman come in and you know you have to have twenty pounds to place and you also got a shot at BIG BASS pot too.

Some one yells "He's got it!"

So far, the biggest fish has been seven (7) pounds.

You get butterflies in your stomach, because when you weighed it on your scale it was nine pounds plus.

But it does not matter until they weigh it officially and you pass the polygraph.

You know every one is watching for you are the last to come in the third wave.

BIG tournament over 350 hard core fishing bass anglers all wanting to win.

You dig into your live well. Pulling out all your fish saving the BIG one for last.

Holy crap! You could win this !

The walk to the scale is a long walk. Your nerves are going crazy until they get your bag and it is like a dream.

You need four (4) ounces to win!

Nobody remembers second place.

They weigh your fish and you have seven ounces over the last top weight total.

Twenty seven pounds, two ounces

27.2 pounds!!!!!

A new Champion on a old lake !

Plus you won BIG BASS pot, at ten dollars each angler put in times 350 entries.

Steak tonight!!

More fun than a barrel of Crappie!!

Bassaholic!

We are sorry to say, there are no cures except get in the water and fish!

Go Early and Stay Late!

Two weeks earlier pre-fishing for the State Championship

It is pouring. Rain and thunderstorms are predicted though out the weekend. You are here with six other Top Ten qualifiers to pre - fish for the State Championship but mother nature has played a joke and has given you the worst conditions to find fish and give you some insight on why, when, where and how you are going to plan to win and place in the top twenty.

You know from past experience that the sponsors only pay attention to the top twenty and offers do not come as easy as people think. You have to work and learn the marketing game of the outdoors and be around the right people.

My partner was a born Louisiana Coon ass and could fish the socks off anybody I know. He was one of the Top Six from his club and this was his 7th State Championship to qualify.

His name was St. Joe and he was gruff, but a die hard tournament Bass Fisherman!

So St. Joe and I met at the ramp at 4:00 am and talked our smack, put our rain gear on and Motorcycle helmet, back the Ranger into the water and headed out.

We could not fish for it was hard, hard rain coming down. But, this was conditioning our mind in case the tournament has bad weather.

We slowly pulled out into the basin that led to the river that led to the lake we found flying over the area to find the holes when the weather was nice five days earlier.

It was still dark and we could not see very well, but St. Joe had a instinct like no other Bass fisherman I know, so we moved forward slowly. Very slow.

My Ranger was tough, but a log from this storm or anything blown in would ruin a practice trip.

We finally made it to the river, still pouring rain and windy, but now it was day light and we could see, so we hit the throttle and made that 200 Mercury work for us.

I know we missed a few stumps and floating logs but St Joe was a seasoned boat man and I trusted him completely!

After a five mile run up river we found the little lake we had saw on the plane trip but there was a problem, the rain had flooded the small creek that led us in and now was a raging river. We had to find another way in.

We backed out and started looking for other ways. I saw a tiny creek but there was a large gap that was waterless to get back into the water that led to the secret lake.

St. Joe said "Let's Jump it"

I said "You are Crazy!!"

He jumped out of the boat and gathered some logs and made a sort of a ramp. He came back to me and said "we will back up and hit the ramp, jump ten feet and land in the water that leads to the lake. We can do it. I betcha dinner "

I looked at him shook my head and put my helmet on and said' "Lets git it"

We backed up fifty or so yards and gunned it, hitting that ramp hard.

It worked!

We went flying and landed in the water, lost a tackle box and the cooler !!

Only problem now - How are we going to get back?

It did not matter. We were in Hog Heaven !!

The rain had cleared up a little and we saw clear water and Lilly pads and there was an added attraction.

We saw four five old duck blinds that we did not know was there and there was a drop off about fifteen feet near the blinds. Too cool!

As I look back I realize that Karate portrayed a major factor in my wins in Bass Events.

I knew what a winner feels like and I knew what a loser feels like too.

I did not like that feeling.

I had my hero's like in Sport Karate - Mike Stone, Ed Parker, John Natividad. Now it was bass fishing icon's Rick Clunn and Roland Martin and of course I had my sponsors in fishing now like in Sport Karate .

There was this one thing that really stood out in my mind and heart. Coming from a home with no family of blood relatives, these people I would meet in Karate events and Bass fishing events were special and they did become my family.

Friends forever.

No other experience has given me that feeling.

Karate and Bass Fishing! Imagine That!

God Bless America and opportunities of life.

The first cast is always the sweetest, but that is another story, of another lake and another sweet morning of tournament Bass Fishing!

Chapter 12
A New Beginning

A New Beginning

As you read this last chapter I hope you have enjoyed my journey and letting me share with you my very humble beginnings, living in a tiny hut in Hawaii and coming to the mainland at the young age of fourteen with nothing but dreams and a Black Belt. It has been a adventure, truly I have meant some incredible persons in and out of martial arts .

Here is the story of one man's influence that would change my life forever and why I have the motivation to succeed in life and to always be there to help others.

One of the big influences on my life was a young man in the clothing business who manage a store in Modesto ,California, his name was Sheridan Beauving and the store was Kaufman's Mens Wear, a high price clothing store that sold Louie Roth, Ratner and Hart Shaffner Marx suits and Nunn Bush shoes, he drove a 911 red Porsche and was married to the most beautiful lady I have ever seen.

I was in the park one day working out kicking trees and I notice he was watching me, finally he walked over and ask me what I was doing, it was the early seventies and martial arts wasn't very popular, the Billy Jack movie and Bruce Lee movies was about it as far as mass appeal.

I said to him **'This is called Karate, Japanese Karate"** I then showed him a Kata and he was fascinated.

He asked if he was to old to learn and of course I said "No" and it was a start of a friendship that would last for years.

After a year of private training, one day he asked me if I was I happy at the little store I worked at selling electronic equipment, I wasn't really in fact I was bored out of my mind.

He asked me if I knew about commission sales, I didn't, so that day he offered me job at his store.

I showed up in a week as he asked me to do in the most expensive to me finest J C Penny suit I could buy on my budget, I paid two hundred dollars, new shoes, new belt and I bought three ties thinking I would look different each day wearing a different tie.

I had to buy all this stuff with my rent money and eat peanut butter sandwiches for breakfast lunch and dinner, occasionally I could afford a hamburger, but that was rare and far in between the little paychecks, with rent, insurance, lights and other overhead I thought Macaroni and cheese was a delicacy, a gourmet meal!

I showed up at nine o'clock and I notice everyone looking at me strange, Sheridan walked up to me and said "Why are you dressed up? Everyone starts in the basement selling jeans and casual wear for the first six to eight months and if you make your quota you will be promoted to the sales floor ". Man, I was embarrassed but still eager to learn the new game of commission sales.

Six months go by and I make double my quota and more money I have ever imagined and Sheridan calls me up stairs to the main office sits me down and tells me he is going to teach me now the art of soft sale and with a little polishing I would make a fine clothing salesman.

In three years time I am in the Top five salesman on the floor and the last Christmas I worked for him I sold over twenty thousand dollars in sales with a commission check over seven thousand dollars in my account, I had learned the art of soft sale and was ready to take on the world.

I tell this story only because that is what I am doing now and will do in the future when it becomes necessary to share with the public and media about our pioneers and legends of Sport Karate, it is soft sales that gets into the news offices, television stations and media, they all care about football, baseball, tennis even ping pong gets more media coverage than pure martial arts.

The **Museum of Sport Karate** is a soft sale project, you know it's there, you want to support it but because it has never been exposed, you just accept it, well here is a hard fact my braddahs, men and ladies who are our pioneers and legends that were born in the 1940's, we are losing them to life, let alone to accidents or illness's and we better do something now.

I was asked to support two of our living treasures in Martial arts though a school business plan called America's Best under **Master Buddy Hudson**, the two living treasures are **Grand Master Jhoon Rhee** age eighty plus, the father of American Tae Kwon Do and Blood and Gut legend **Grand Master J. Pat Burleson** seventy-five years young, both are incredible martial artist and were personal friends of mine before I decided to be come the National Sales Director for **America's Best school Business Plans.**

Together with the **Museum of Sport Karate** I feel **America's Best** will help take martial art studios into the twenty-first century in sales and motivation; and with it the media public eye to help this new generation see what I saw and felt fifty years ago back in Hawaii when I threw my first punch and kick.

The art of Karate!

The art of the soft sale!

Two partners with one goal in mind!

Words From Legends And Peers

Words From Legends And Peers

DUANE R. ETHINGTON'S OPENING SPEECH FOR THE SPORTS KARATE HISTORY MUSEUM

We've come a long way, babe!

From the spawning of the very first dojo in America through the britches-busting youthful exuberance of the Texas "blood and guts" era and into today's strapping grown-up rambunctious version, Sports Karate has become a rousing success. But how did it arrive at this point and why has it been so successful?

A very few realize that martial arts in America began way back in 1848 with the arrival of the Chinese Coolies who were brought in to work on the railroads. These 'imports' secretly practiced versions of Kung Fu.

Then came judo, introduced by Yoshiaki Yamashita in 1902 and Kali in 1907 by Jack Santos. In 1921 America got its first wide-spread exposure to oriental martial arts in a movie called THE OUTSIDE WOMAN. Throughout the years every other aspect of martial arts has been brought to America's shores.

Closer to home, perhaps, after Mas Oyama traveled in 32 states giving his famous demonstration of chopping the horns off live and charging bulls, Robert Trias became the first documented Caucasian to open a school in America. He opened in Phoenix, Arizona in 1946 and founded the United States Karate Association the next year. Collegiate judo flourished and Edward Kaloudis introduced karate to the east coast about the same time that Ed Parker was bringing Kenpo to Provo, Utah.

Master Trias held the first organized tournament in 1955 and Korean Jhoon Rhee opened shop in San Marcos, Texas. Rhee's class, which spawned legendary Allen Steen, the 'Father of Texas Karate', was probably the beginning of the 'Blood and Guts' era.

J. Pat Burleson became the first 'National Karate Champion' and Allen Steen made martial arts history by defeating Chuck Norris and Joe Lewis, back to back at Ed Parker's International Tournament in 1966. It was a feat never before accomplished.

Other greats across the nation were making their marks, as well. Thomas LaPuppett, Louis Delgado, Don Nagle, George Mattson, S. Henry Cho and Peter Urban were leading the east coast while, Ed Parker, Chuck Norris, Joe Lewis, Steve Armstrong, Bong Yu, Ernie Reyes, Bruce Lee and Mike Stone, who was perhaps the greatest tournament competitor of all time were handling things nicely on the west coast.

Texans were dominating wherever they appeared. Skipper Mullins, David Moon, Chuck Loven, Fred Wren, Roy Kurban, Demetrius Havanas, Harold Gross, Jim Harkins, Jim Miller, James Butin, Ed Daniels and Linda Denley were putting their special stamps on the sport that would stand for all time.

Texans, though, weren't the only pioneers as Mike Stone, Jim Harrison, Ken Knudson, Joe Lewis, Benny Urquidez, Ernie Reyes, Bill Wallace, Howard Jackson, Joe Corley, Keith Vitali, Glenn Keeney, Roger Carpenter, Jerry Peddington, Steve Fisher and Pat and John Worley along with Jeff Smith and Ron Marcini were elevating the sport in their respective areas.

Fighters, though, weren't the only ones to make their marks and perpetuate this ever-growing, strapping youth known as Sport Karate. Magazine editors, writers and promoters all had a hand in making the sport an elite entity. Mito Uyhara, Howard Hanson, Renardo Barden, Al Weiss, John Corcoran, Mike Anderson, Emile Farkas, Duane Ethington, Gary Lee, Fumio Demura, Keith Yates, Curtis Wong, Ken Knudson and many others kept the sport growing and in the public eye.

Hollywood did its part, too. Great Martial Artists like Bruce Lee, Bong Soo Han, Chuck Norris, Jean Claude Van Damme, Dolph Lundgren, Philip and Simon Rhee, James Cagney, Yul Brynner, Jackie Chan, Howard Jackson, Tom Laughlin, Benny Urquidez, Mike Stone, Steve Fisher, Sonny Chiba, Jet Li and Tadashi Yamashita lent their particular expertise to filmdome.

Non-martial artists, too, portrayed martial artists. People like Eric Roberts, Sean Connery, Wesley Snipes, David Carridine, Ralph Maccio, Pat Morita and many others were involved.

The great ladies of the sport, too, cannot be overlooked. Graciela Casillas, Linda Denley, Phyllis Evetts, Joy Turberville, Jenice Miller, Malaia DeCastos, Karyn Turner, Charlotte Hoffman, Marion Bermudes, Cynthia Rothrock, Arlene Limas, Lana Hyde, Barbara Nagel, Mary Ann Corcoran and so many others lent beauty and grace to the sport.

Countless others must be recognized, as well. The Raymond McCallum's, Troy Dorsey's, Tim Kirby's, Sean Ethington's, Mark Wendell's, Ishmael Robles', James Toney's, Mike Proctor's, Shannon Harvey's, and Lio Zapata's have all helped to pave the way.

Now here we are. A big, strapping, much admired, talented and here-forever young stalwart who is just about to get our own History Museum and Library and take our rightful place in the world of sports forever more.

From the top of the workhorse chain – the Gary Lee's and Shawn Flanagans – to all the countless people who contributed what they could here and there, American Sport Karate could not and would not BE without you.

A heartfelt thank you and Ous.

Duane Ethington

A STATEMENT FROM SID CAMPBELL, AN AMERICAN SPORT KARATE PIONEER

Aloha and welcome,

The Sport Martial Arts Museum Organization under the guidance of founder Gary Lee is a major step forward in preserving the past, unifying the present and strengthening the future of the sporting aspects of our art. It is also the official home of the history, traditions and accomplishments of great martial artists that pioneered the way in bringing these exciting sport-oriented martial traditions to the United States and spreading it throughout the western world.

What we see today in the vast expanse where the martial arts have entrenched itself in American's culture and social fabric is a plethora of positive human qualities that was spawned by the martial arts sport movement.

Through venues like karate tournaments, major action-adventure motion picture productions, professionally sanctioned televised events, martial arts schools, law enforcement agency defense tactics curriculum, Internet connectivity, seminars, magazine publishers, equipment supply companies, instructional books, educational DVDs, video arcade games, etc. — can all, in one way or another, trace its roots back to the sport martial arts competitors of the early 1960s when the Asian martial traditions were being introduced to the world. More specifically, it was the martial arts competitors, tournament producers and the fans of that bygone era that we today call the "golden age" of karate in America is of where this expansive and phenomenal growth evolved from in the first place.

Being fortunate enough to be one of the first Americans to teach Okinawan karate in the United States and western world during karate's "golden age" of the 60s, I was blessed to be a part this cultural evolution. To be a small part of this dedicated cadre of this movement which now touts tens of millions of practitioners on a global scale still humbles me beyond the scope of words alone.

In my wildest dreams I could not have imagined that the martial disciplines like karate, kung-fu (gung-fu), judo, jujitsu, ninjitsu, tae kwon do, kempo, escrima, kendo, aikido, iaido, kali, capoeira, savate, sambo, kobudo, pankration, bugei, wushu, mixed martial arts and eclectic martial arts would have reached that level of popularity in the past forty some odd years. And, to see the art I love so much endure these sometimes tumultuous times and undergo so many innovative changes along the way while still retaining the quintessential essence of its original purpose and traditional values is truly astounding.

Perhaps what is just incredible about this form of physical expression that emphasizes moral and ethical values is that it has helped develop some of the finest human beings that these past four decades of growth can produce. I must attribute this, at least in part, to the exceptional martial arts educators that have dedicated their life and energy to elevating the spirit of the warrior and teaching the arts that has been a way of life for a select few for the past fifteen hundred years.

The Sport Martial Arts Museum was created and founded on the premise that the efforts, dedication, perseverance and enthusiasm of these early practitioners would be preserved and passed forth for posterity sake. A noble cause in deed when we stop to think that many future generations will know who was responsible for this phenomenal growth and worldwide popularity from a sport perspective. Again, I must reiterate that this worthy endeavor to document, archive and house the sporting aspects of these myriad of martial disciplines that were, in part, responsible for this global popularity of the martial arts is the righteous and just action to take so that future generations will be able to share in the excitement, enthusiasm and camaraderie that was unwittingly nurtured in karate's "golden age" of karate in America.

And, as with any endeavor that attracts the interest of millions of avid devotees, preserving the past, unifying the present and strengthening the future needs a strong foundation to insure existence. I believe Gary Lee has set the cornerstone in place through his unceasing efforts and true love for the martial disciplines to guide this endeavor into the future. His insightful perception will undoubtedly insure that the sports aspects of the martial arts will be preserved and passed forward for many, many generations to come. For that, we will all be deeply indebted.

As you visit the Five House you will step back in time to when America and the western world was embracing the cultural traditions of Asia and forming an international bond that is stronger today because of his many years of hard work. Essentially Gary Lee has captured time in a bottle so that others can share these moments and drink from that same fountain of knowledge that America's karate pioneers enjoyed from its introduction in 1945 in Phoenix, Arizona.

With great respect and Aloha,

Malama pono,

Sid Ka'imi Campbell

10th dan, hanshi, kaicho Founder, the World Okinawan Shorin-ryu Karate-do and Kobudo Association (WOSKKA)

Karate grandmaster, artist, author, actor, tournament producer

A STATEMENT FROM A HISTORY GENERAL AND AN UNDEFEATED WORLD KARATE CHAMPION

Aloha Gary,

I commend you on your exceptional efforts to make your dreams come true. Many people have talked of a museum as you envision it but few if any have taken the positive action to make it happen. I wish for you what you wish for all martial artist, a place to reflect and remember our roots and heritage for it is extremely important now more so than ever. I know you will experience much success and happiness and feel great about yourself and what you are doing for all martial artist regardless of system or style. We are all one no matter what our personal preferences in applying our art. I personally want to thank you and what you to know that you have my support in making your dream come true.

With great respect and Aloha,

Mike Stone
Undefeated World Karate Champion

Documents And Certificates

Documents And Certificates

I am including documents and certificates in this book that I think may be of historical or educational interest to Martial Arts students, enthusiasts and historians.

I am hoping some of these will serve as inspiration to motivate coming generations of Martial Artists in their journey to Black Belt and beyond.

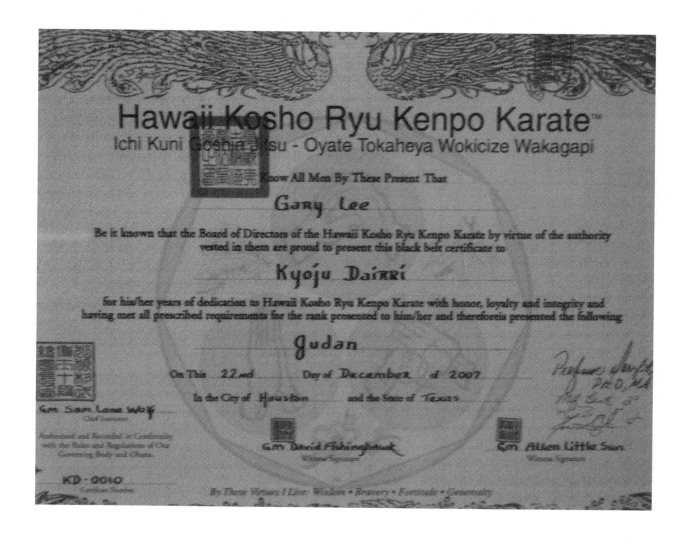

Chinese Karate Federation   Nº 00301

REMAINS DEDICATED TO PRESERVING AND PROMOTING THE MARTIAL ARTS TOWARD THE HIGHEST STANDARDS OF PROFESSIONALISM. TESTING OF ONES PHYSICAL AND INTELLECTUAL PROWESS ARE OF EQUAL MEASURE IN DETERMINING AN INDIVIDUAL'S DEGREE OF PROFICIENCY IN THE "CHINESE KARATE FEDERATION".

Where As On This Day:

STUDENT _MR. GARY LEE_

HAS BEEN TESTED AND PROMOTED TO THE _SAN-DAN_

RANK OF: _3RD DEGREE_ _BLACK BELT_

THE ABOVE STUDENT DEMONSTRATED AND MET ALL REQUIREMENTS MANDATORY HAS ON THIS DAY PHYSICAL, MENTAL, AND ETHICAL FOR PROMOTION IN THE "CHINESE KARATE FEDERATION".

DATED AND APPROVED ON THIS _ELEVENTH_ DAY OF _JULY_, IN THE YEAR OF _1982_. THIS BOARD HAS BEEN HELD AT THE TOWN OF _CHICAGO_, AND THE STATE OF _ILLINOIS_.

THIS CERTIFICATE IS NOT VALID UNLESS SIGNED BY THE OFFICIAL GOVERNING BODY OF THE "CHINESE KARATE FEDERATION".

THE GOVERNING BODY HAVE WITNESSED AND APPROVED THE ABOVE:

Jack D. Farr — STUDENT'S INSTRUCTOR — Degree Black Belt

NAME — C.K.F. DIRECTOR — Degree Black Belt

Rick Fowler — STATE OF THE ARTS — IV Degree Black Belt

Dan Anderson — HONORABLE WITNESS — III Degree Black Belt

World Registry Of Black Belts Martial Arts Organizations, Federations & Associations

Be it hereby known that:

Gary Lee 8th Dan Okinawan Karate

Is a Registered member of the WRBBOF. Ranks and the dates of study, following our research appear to be authentic and correct.

I, therefore, affix my signature on this,

the 27 day of July, 2009

Member ID: WR5041

Signature of Board member

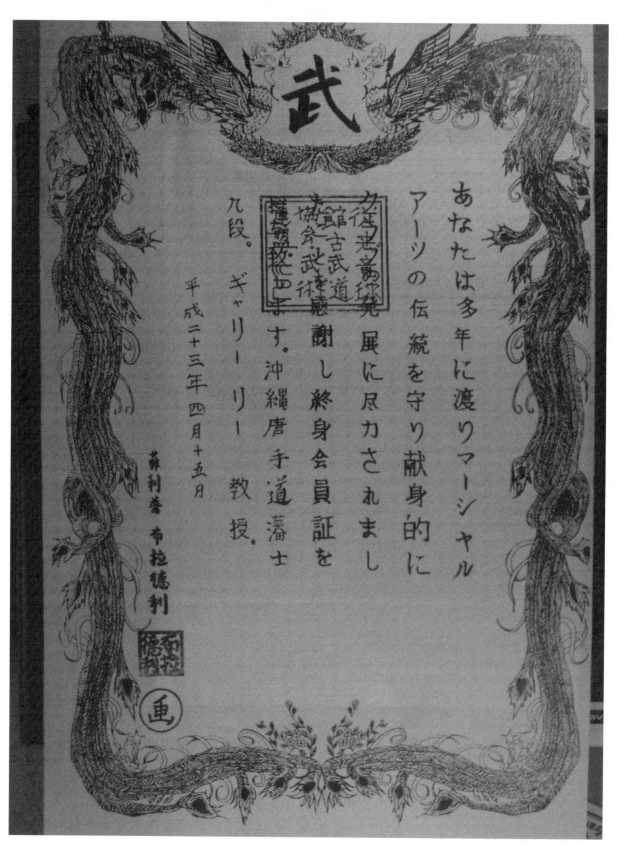

Traditional Okinawan Kobudo Association and Martial Arts Federation

Founder & Chief Instructor: Phil Bradley 07807648084
Secretary: Lisa Hammond 07596 799018

従来竜球館古武道協会.
武術連盟.

27/4/2011

Dear Sir,

It gives me the greatest pleasure to present to you this Award. The Japanese Caligraphy is hand brushed by myself and reads from right to left as follows:

"The Lifetime Membership Award, for long and dedicated service to Preserving the History of Martial Arts", presented to - Okinawan Karate do Hanshi 9th Dan Professor Gary Lee. Dated 15/4/2011 being the date you excepted the Award. and signed and stamped with family seal. Philip Bradley.

Sir i remain yours in Martial Arts.

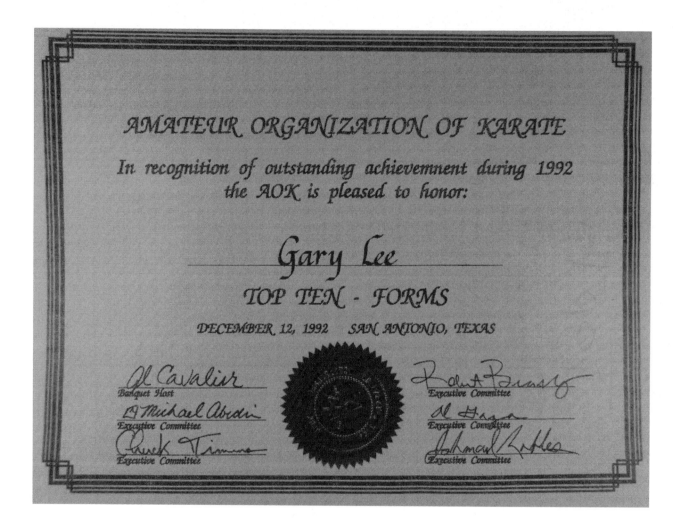

AMERICAN BLACK BELT ACADEMY

July 29, 1983

Mr. Mark Gutche
Del Monte Corporation
One Market Plaza
Room 1329
San Francisco, CA 94105

Dear Sir:

I am honored to have the opportunity to write this letter of recommendation for Mr. Gary Lee. I have watched Mr. Lee evolve into a dominate force in Texas karate competition both as an athlete and a trainer of athletes. I know that Gary Lee could test his skills on a national level with your sponsorship. Mr. Lee's Hawaiian heritage would certainly lend itself to your product as would his credibility as a martial artist.

As a member of the Black Belt Hall of Fame, and a former world-ranked professional fighter, I have had the opportunity to observe many fine competitors in the sport of karate. Gary is among the best. If I can be of further assistance, please call.

Respectfully,

Roy D. Kurban

RDK/jk

May 6, 1984

To Whom It May Concern:

    I am writing this letter in reference to one of the contract shows at Astroworld for 1984, Gary Lee's Texas Karate All Star Show. Gary Lee contacted Astroworld and proposed a show package during January, 1984. After working with him on his ideas and explaining exactly what Astroworld was looking for in a show, Gary Lee developed an outstanding, family entertainment-style show for the park. The show is fifteen minutes in length, and pre-taped with background music. There are four different show formats which may be rotated throughout the day.

    As a performer, Gary does an outstanding job, exhibiting quality entertainment and showmanship. He and his all stars work well with the crowd. Gary brings children and adults of all ages in to his show to perform and works well with all of them. They provide the level of entertainment and dedication to their performance above and beyond what is expected of them. It has been a pleasure working with Gary, and his all stars. I wish him all the success in future endeavors, and recommend him to perform in any environment or situation which may come his way.

Sincerely,

Patsy Albers
Show Operations Coordinator

NATIVIDAD KARATE AND KICKBOXING ASSOCIATION
P.O. BOX 60335
LAS VEGAS, NEVADA 89160
natividadkarate@msn.com

Professor Gary Lee
C/o Museum of Sport Karate
13313 South West Free Way, Suite 210
Sugar Land, Texas 77478

Professor Lee:

As per your request and I am honored to do this, I enclose an autograph top, an autographed photo, a short brief video of me demonstrating some kicks (made by one of my students) and a little booklet (also made by a student). I hope they are of use to use to you.

I thank you for including me in such honored and prestigious group.

You are the person that keeps the traditions and legends alive. The power in you pen is more powerful than what we did individually because you keep the stories and legends alive for past, present and future to connect with forever in time. There can not be a present without the past and there can never be a future with the present and past being connected.

I thank you for your achievements, your dreams and your visions.

John Natividad

Home of Martial Arts

September 10, 2004

Hawaii State Sport Hall of Fame:

This is a letter of recommendation for Gary Lee to be inducted into the "Hawaii State Sport Hall of Fame," for his vast amount of accomplishments and dedication to the Martial Arts.

I've had the privilege of knowing Gary Lee for about eight years. It started with the involvement of my project "Home of Martial Arts." Over the past eight years Gary Lee has assisted us with this project with his great ability to network with a variety of very influential people and has demonstrated his immense amount of passion toward building a place to represent the history of all Martial Arts.

Gary came from Hawaii with almost nothing, worked extremely hard, and proved himself as a fantastic champion in tournament competition. He has also created the "Living Legends," in which great kickboxing champions are awarded and recognized for their accomplishments in history. Gary has worked with and dedicated a large amount of time to children, giving them seminars to improve their lives by using Martial Arts. Gary has also created the concept of having a banquet and "Roast" of exceptional Martial Art legends and has hosted many of these "Roasts."

In the eight years that I've know Gary Lee, I have seen a real champion and a man with the largest heart for his fellow humans and the Martial Arts. Gary has paid his dues all through his life time and I highly recommend that he be inducted in the "Hawaii State Sport Hall of Fame" for his vast amount of accomplishments and dedication. He is truly a man of high honor and extremely deserving of this induction.

Thank you for your consideration.

Sincerely,

William J. Berry
Chairman-CEO

William J. Berry, Chairman-CEO • 2306 Edwards Road • Waterloo, NY 13165
Phone: 1-315-539-9601

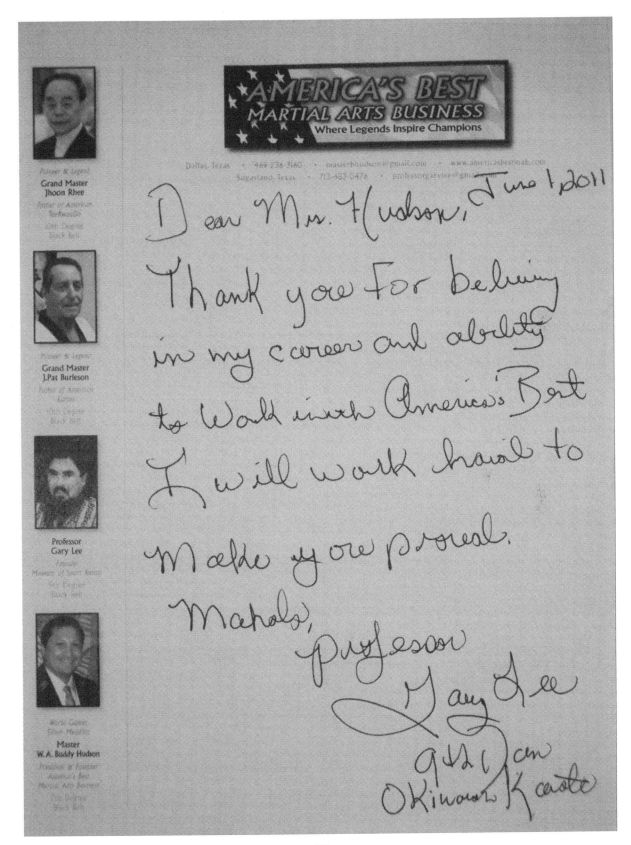

Notes From My Diary

Notes From My Diary

Here are some notes from my diary. The comments and autographs of legendary Martial Artists contained in it have inspired me through the years. See if you can find your hero, your friend, your teacher or your role model below. I hope these pages inspire you for years.

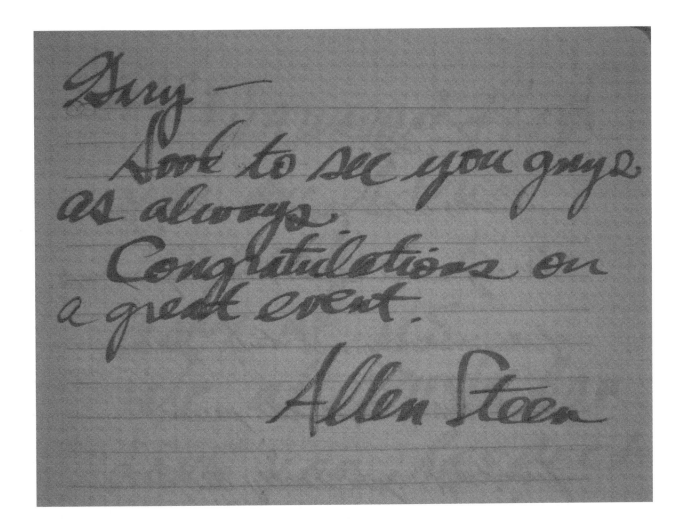

No Nothing is more pleasing to an old time martial artist than to share a moment with a dedicated and true to the martial arts. Such as you — Gary Lee — I love you and will always support your endeavors —

Love In Christ,
Ronnie Al, 9th Dan
Rio Grande Valley — Texas

To Master Lee,

It is such a pleasure + honor to be in your presence + attend your son's exam. Look forward to the LLRB Nationals. You will always be in my thoughts + prayers.

Mr Lee, you are a true martial artist. Some persons take the arts + some are the martial arts. You are one of the honorable + true martial artist.

God Bless you + be with you always

James Toney 9th Dan

Master Lee,

Every-so-often there is an individual who comes along & makes a true difference in this world.

You are such a person & everyone seems to agree.

I am very honored to have been included in your "Living Legends" Ceremony & to sit on your son, Garret's, exam board.

Always, feel free to call on me for anything you think I can help you with.

Many thanks!

— Richard Jenkins, 9th Dan

Gary —

What you've put on here is truly a multi-generational event! Congratulations and here's to many more.

"Super Dan"
Anderson

24 Sep 95

P.S. It's nice to be back in the true home of the ridge hand!

Gary,

After all of the miles traveled, all of the awards won, the one thing that we cherish are the relationships that we have cultivated. It is amazing how far mutual respect is developed for a lifetime because of a positive spirit and love for a common activity. For years as competitors, although not head to head, a kind word and smile has formed a bond between us that will last the rest of our lives.

Thanks for the memories and let's make sure that the next generation has as much fun as we did!!

Richard Plowden

Gary,

It was a true inspiration having you in my corner at the last Super Brawl of the millennium. I truly appreciate the coaching and the personal friendship, you really are a true friend.

Your friend and Collegue

Tom Wasinger

THOMAS WASINGER

GARY:
Hawaiian flash
you are a true
inspiration to so
many of us.
We, at Bushi-Ban
love you, respect
and very much
Admire you!!

Love Always
Zuhair Hillail

12-18-99

Gary,

Karate has been one of the high lights of my life. The people, events the study of an art that develops the mind body and spirit. I think back over the past 38 years and all the wonderful things that have happen to me and the martial arts. The great and caring people I have met over the years such as Pat Johnson, Bill Wallace Bob Wall & Gary Lee to name a few.

I'm writing this at the 1999 Super Grand World Games in Niagara Canada. This whole week has been impressive. I'm looking forward to the day when Karate will take it place with other great sports.

To Gary Lee, a positive force in the art of Karate

Carson Hurley

CARSON HURLEY

Master Lee 9-24-99
— Gary, my friend —
The spirit of the Samurai still lives.
You are living proof of that.
Thank you for including me among your friends.
Tim Vought

Dear Mr. Lee, 9-24-99

What a fine job you've done with Garrett; he's done you Texas proud today.

love,
Marian Kirby

Dear Garrett,

I want to tell you again what an excellent job you did on your Black Belt test. I hope you take to heart all that the masters on your board told you & will use that wisdom throughout your life.

Lots of love to you,
Marian Kirby

To: Gary Lee

To a great spirited person with a true meaning of the Martial Arts way.

Your smiling face always cheers those of us up that have a bad day.

Our goal in Martial Arts is to work with our own community to help the youth of today so we can all have a better tomorrow.

Keep up the good work and always keep that smile

"May God Bless you"

Jerry

Jerry & Pamela Lemmons

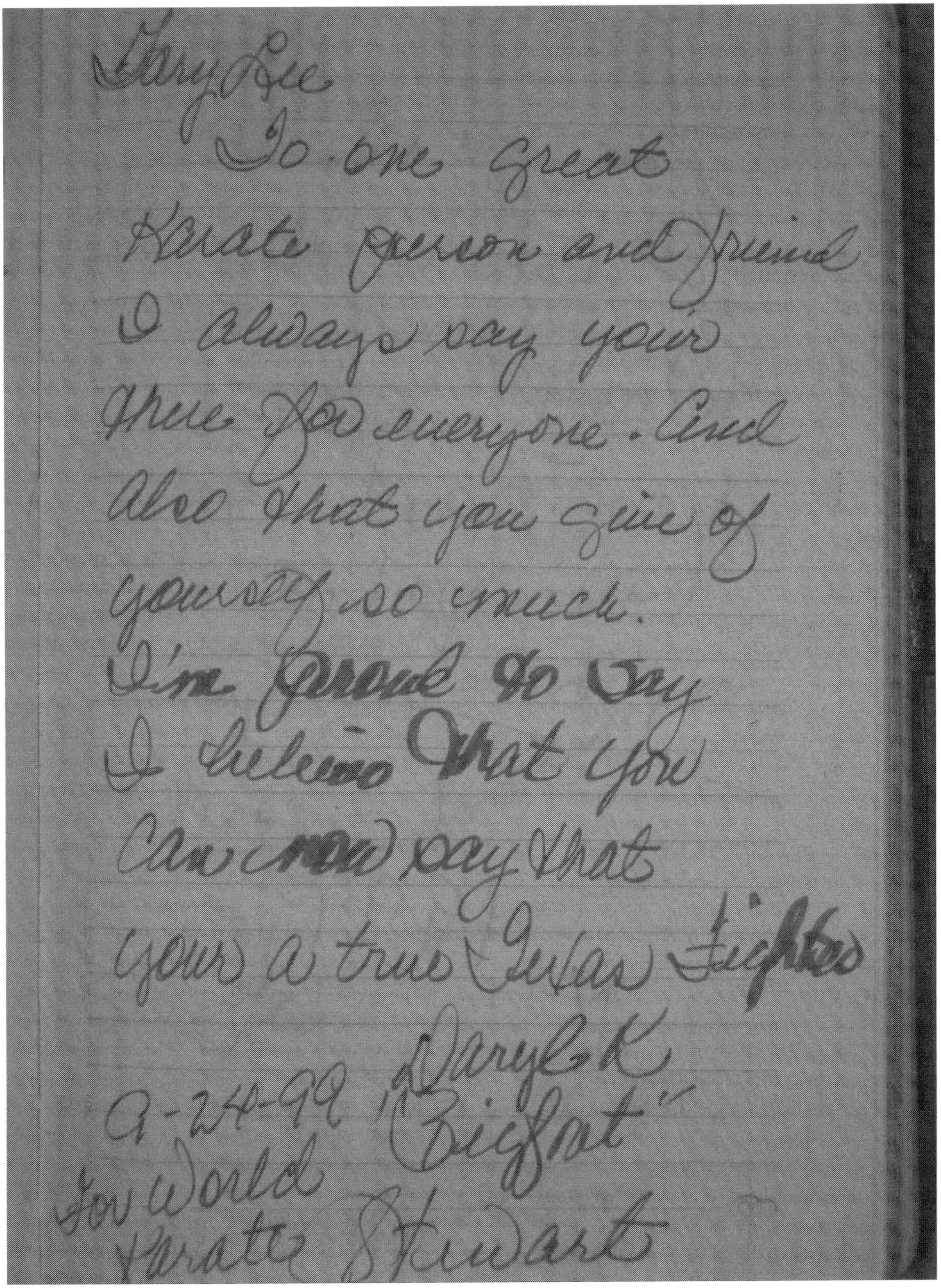

Gary Lee,
   To one great Karate person and friend I always say your true for everyone. And also that you give of yourself so much. I'm proud to say I believe that you can now say that your a true Texan fighter

9-24-99   Daryl K
           "Bigfoot"
For World
Karate Stewart

Gary,

You did very good on your test, I was very impressed. Keep up with your karate career and before long, you will be the No 1 karate fighter in the world.

Danny Bergeron
Hachi Dan

From Gato,

You have done a great job in their promotion and enjoyed your sons test. Thank you for invite me! May the Lord bless you and your family!

Jim "Soto"
Salas

Gary Lee,

The martial arts is a life long journey. If you're lucky, along the way you meet fellow martial artists & forge lasting bonds of friendship. Whether past, present or future the opportunity to compete, train and learn from these fellow travelers only helps to make the journey that much more enjoyable and rewarding.

Mike Shintaku
Moo Duk Kwan Tang Soo Do

To Gary & Garrett,
Thanks for inviting me to share this special day for the two of you. Garrett your dad has never been so proud as he is today. Gary you are a great dad and promoter of the arts. God Bless you both and I look forward to seeing your future's develop.

Al Garza

To Shihan Lee,
Thank for inviting me. Hope to do business with you and all the Black Belts here in Texas.
Sincerely,
Shorihe bromi Palalon
Asing-I Ohwan

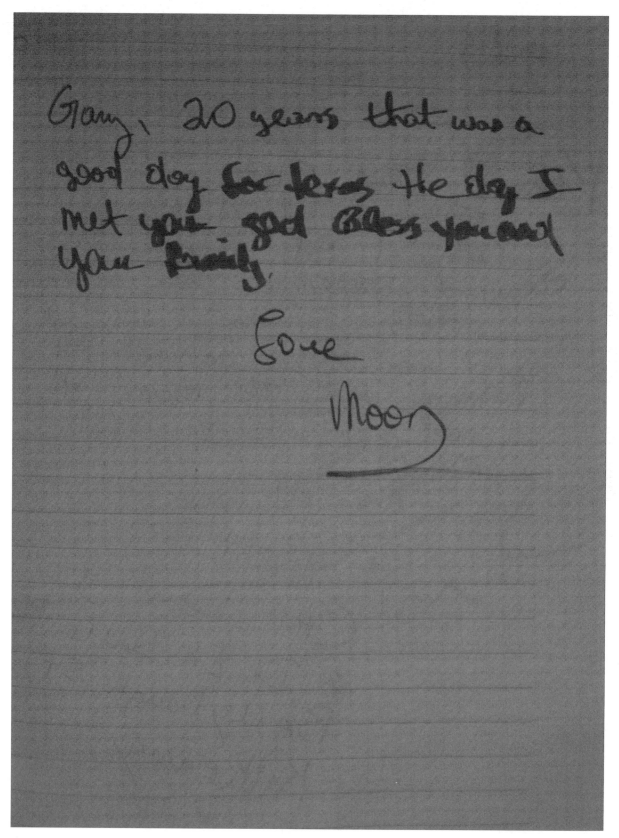

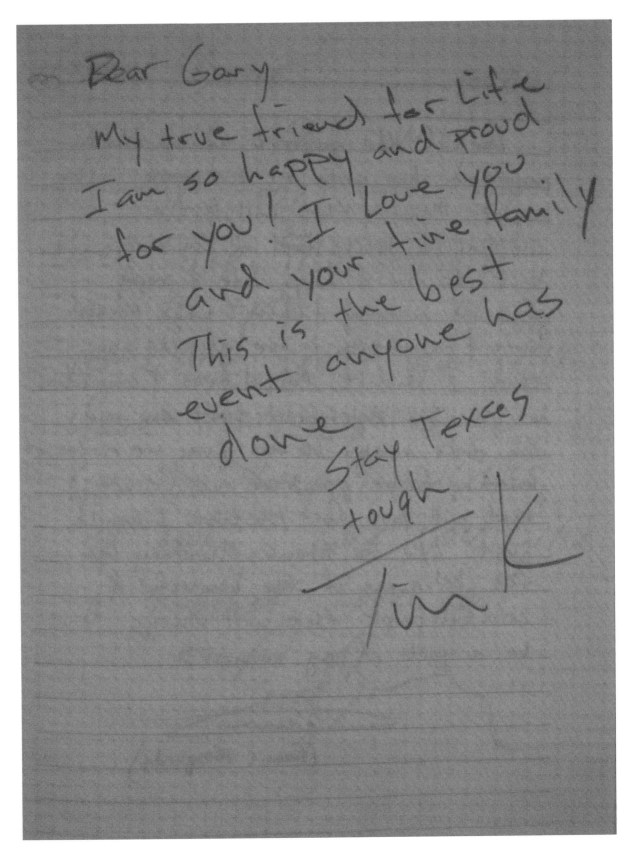

Gary

One of the greatest things that competition has given me are great memories. Memories that will last a lifetime. I believe we all try our best to live a happy life & people find it in many different ways. Martial arts & competition is one of the ways that I did it. Martial Arts & competition has given me experiances that no one can take away. It has given me excitement, something to be proud of and friends that will last for lifetime. I would just like to thank Mr. Gary Lee for being one of the wonderful & colorful people that will always be a part of my memories

(Ramie Mosqueda)

Gray & Garret
I love yall with all my Heart you have Been Like my Second Dad to me over the years and Grett we still Have many years to Go So keep the kicks up and I love you Like a Brother Love yall

Perry B

Dear Gary —

It's been a long road, it's been a great story! I am proud to call you my friend and respect what you have brought to Texas Martial Arts. I wish you and yours the very best in life. Peace, Health to you.

Your friend — Shawn C. Wilson
99 Pai Lum Tao

Gary — Over the years you have continued to work hard to make sure the history and the people that made Texas Karate the finest & toughest in the nation be remembered. Thank you for all you do.

Shawn Wilson

Dear Gary,

I do not feel I have made enough Martial Arts accomplishments to be in this book. There are many more prominent people in our Industry who have helped it become what it is today. Some good and some bad. However I will compliment the leaders in the Sport as well as the business section who have pioneered it as a whole. Many thanks to Gary Lee who is one of those pioneers. Someone who embodies the true Spirit of the arts. Someone who is a fellow brother in Kenpo, and whom I call a friend

Mark Russo

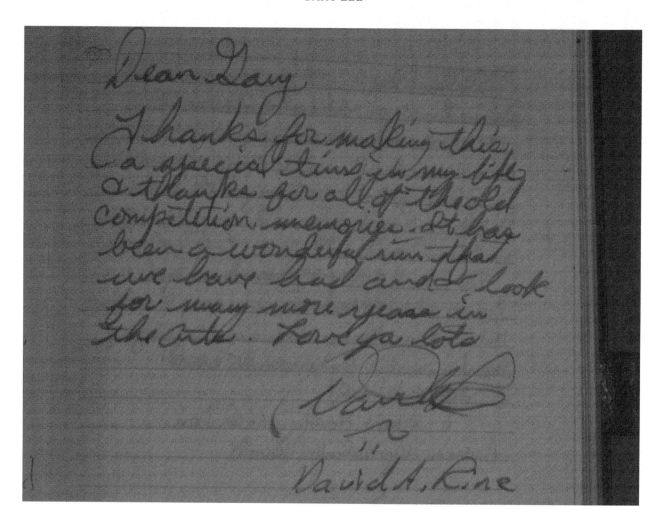

Shihan Wong — It has been such a pleasure to meet you. I did not think I would be able to find people with the true spirit of old time Karate here in Houston. Was I wrong! You would have been right at home training with Sensei Don Buck! I look forward to many years of sweating and training with you.

Thank you for the privilege of participating in Jarrett's Black Belt test. It was awesome to see Jarrett's test and to see the incredible assemblage of legendary masters that were on his board!

Let's work hard!

Calvin Horton, 4th Dan
American Kyokushinkai Karate

Mr Lee,

THE ENTIRE EVENT AND EVENING last Saturday was quite a success. I really enjoyed being included AND having a chance to compete. It was also a pleasure hearing all the "roasts" and to see how all your friends respect and love you. You must be very proud

PAT DUGGAN

Ever since then, Mr. Lee you have been nothing but an inspiration for me.

Even though I was to young to be considered a Texas legend, bringing the living legends the way you did, and allowing me to perform, to show the legends that Texas is still alive and Kicking.

Mr. Lee,
From my heart, thank you for being an inspiration, and most of all a friend.

Gary L. Carico

Well, what can I say? You mean a lot to me. Your kindness is a statement of true friendship. Your martial arts ability sets my standards! Your sincerity is something many blackbelts only wishes for. You are something. Keep being like that!
I love you.

Dewey Earwood

GARY!!
   I HAVE KNOWN YOU SINCE 1994 SUPER GRANDS! YOU HAVE ALWAYS BEEN SO UPLIFTING & SUPPORTIVE OF ME! FOR THIS I THANK YOU!!

   BRIAN PEDA
   "TEAM <u>GOD'S</u> SQUAD"

Gary,

   I owe karate a great debt for all it has done for me in my life. <u>Karate</u> owes you a great deal for all you've done to help it become an art with dignity. Thank you!

   Your friend,
   Pat Johnson

Gary,

Although we haven't met until most recently, I feel I have known you for many years. Your dedication to the Martial Arts is endless. I'm looking forward to a great relationship in the future.

Your Friend
In the Martial Arts

Don Rodrigues

Gary,
  Boy! We go back! Just think what stories we could tell. You are such a presence anywhere you are. Your beacon shines like the lighthouse of the world. Thanks for the wonderful years and all the great memories. Friends forever!

  Harry Dillingham

Master Lee—

Thanks for always being kind & stickin' to the basics!

Your innate ability to "do the right thing" is the greatest asset of all in today's harried pace!!

Love,
Janette Kinham, D.C.

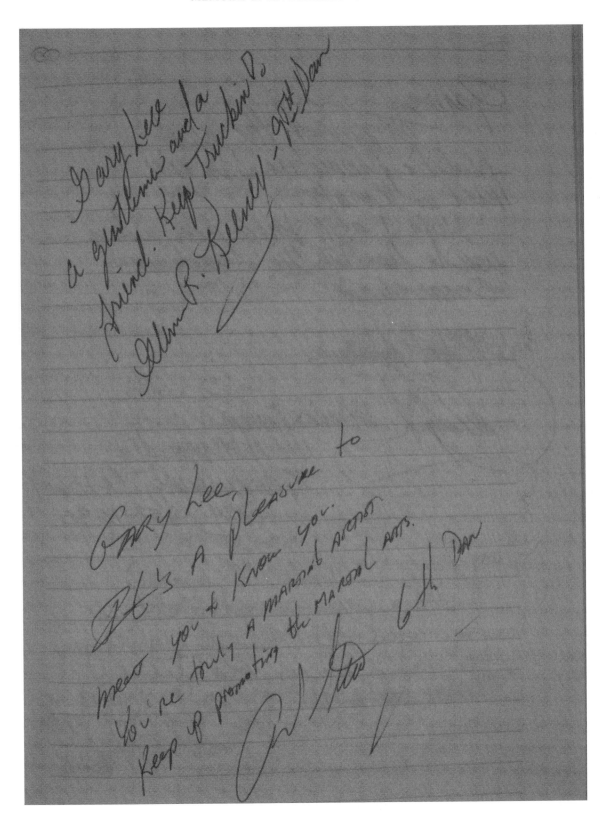

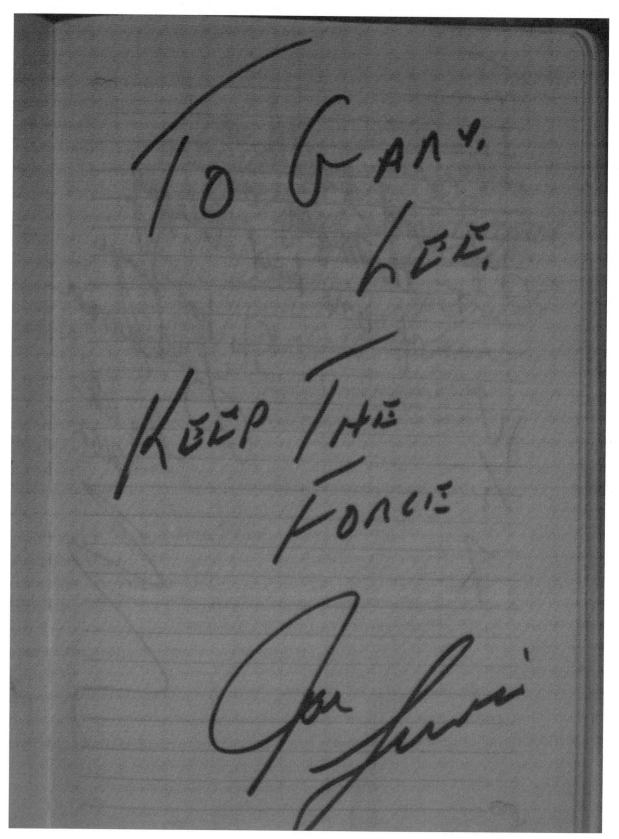

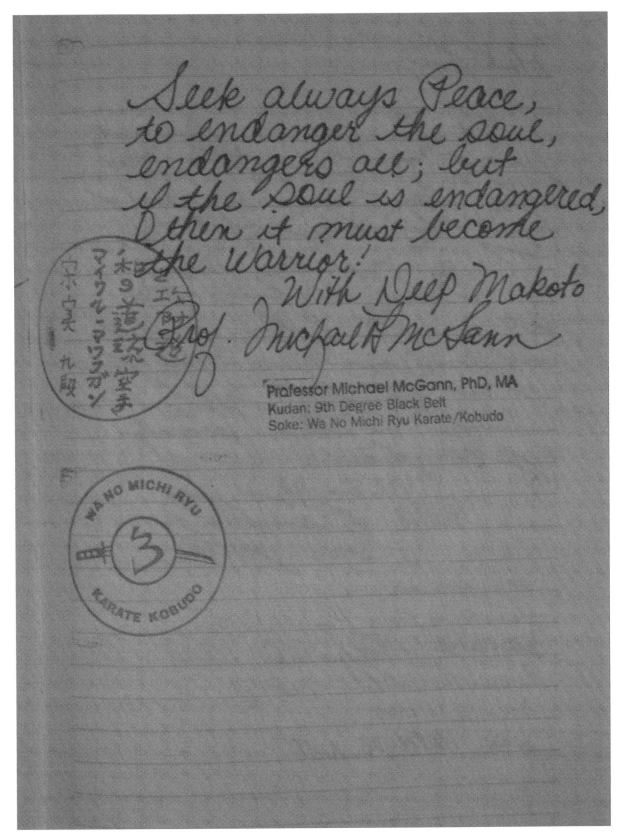

Seek always Peace,
to endanger the soul,
endangers all; but
if the soul is endangered,
then it must become
the warrior!
With Deep Makoto
Prof. Michael McGann

Professor Michael McGann, PhD, MA
Kudan: 9th Degree Black Belt
Soke: Wa No Michi Ryu Karate/Kobudo

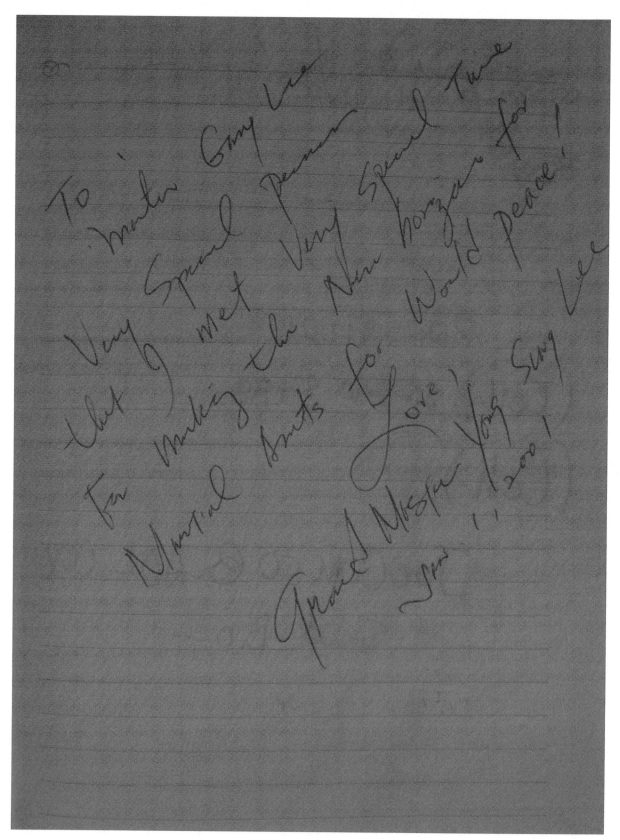

To: Gary Lee
Martin Gary Lee
Very Special Person
that I met Very Special Time
For making the New horizons for
Martial Arts for World Peace!
Love, Sung
Grand Master Young Sung Lee
Sept 11, 2001

Dearest Friend Gary

　We have crossed many paths and obstacles in our life, but our friendship and brotherhood has always been unique. We have now entered into 4 decades of friendship.
　and I am looking forward to many more years of our awesome Legacy in motion.

　　　　　Friends
　　　　　　&
　　　　Renegades 4 ever
　　　　Tony Lopez

　　　　New Years day
　　　　　2001
　　　　Atlanta Airport

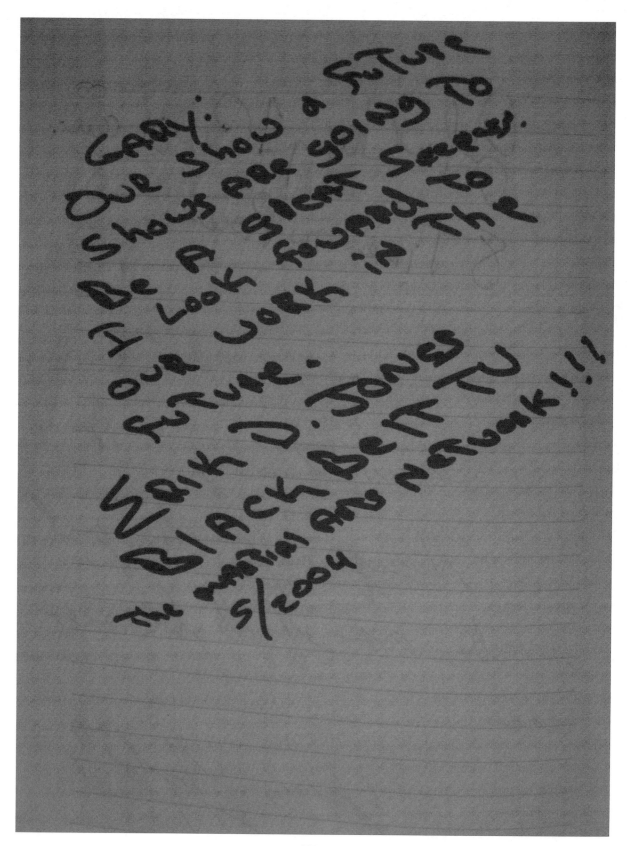

To Butch Lee,

Aloha, I wish you many more years of success in our industry. May your journey be navigated by your shinning star and God be with you.

Peace be with you!

Kawika Kalomoa Burns
David Burns

Gary –

Out of all the people I know in martial arts, you are the one I respect + love the most. I lost my father 2 days before I won my first ever tournament and there has been a huge hole in my world since. You my brother have filled alot of that hole. I have been blessed to know and be associated with you + Garret. You guys are more than family and my life is better because of you.

Love you Bro!

Keep Kickin,
Master Billy W. Swinney

Lil Brother 4-15-2011

Through the years I have watched you grow from a little man to an outstanding Heavy Weight Martial Artest. From your Living Legend Black Belt Test to Arnolds Event with Wesley to Mr Steen's and Mr. Norris's Birthday to Mr Burlson's B-Day we have been together. I am so proud of who you are and have become and what you stand for. You are our future.

Love & Respect OUS.

Patrick Breck Mills

To Professor Gary Lee

Thank you so much for your friendship. You are such an inspiration. I look so forward to our future together.

Master
Buddy Hutton

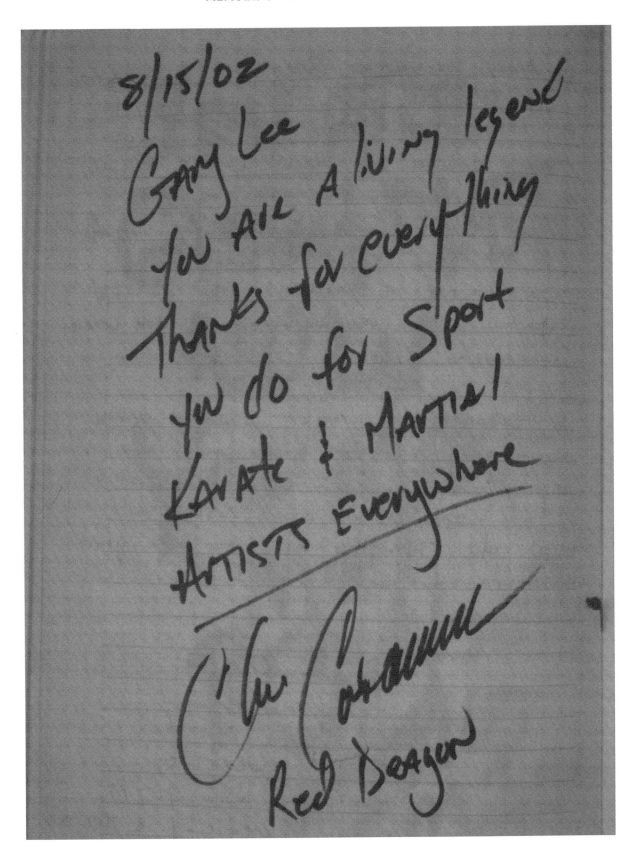

How it bee at first you was a cop to me. But you was a like my Dad bra. I can see him in you! I hope we can hook me up whit life!

Love, you bee.
Mike Yuron

Mr Lee,
It was another great Super Grands, great to see & work with you
Mike Shintaku
11-30-03

Gary,

Hoomana nui i ka maika loa

George Querusu

Lukahu,
Aloha kakou!
Welcome home
Best Wishes,

Mike Young
Master, Kusho Ryu / Kajukenbo

Gary,
Please keep in touch
Best Wishes
Ken Lowe

GARY LEE

Gary —

Although the journey is more important than the destination — its always good to have a visionary destination.

Keith Wyatt

Gary

There are very few people that have a heart of gold. Keep up the good work

Lots of Love

Kenn Kletne

Gary Lee — 8/4/02

It was a pleasure to meet you —
Red Dragon Karate (Clarence)
Wayne E. Divins
World Bo Champion

P.S. Keep up the Hard Work for the Martial Arts.

Gary Lee —

Thank you for your Contribution and Kindness — It is an honor to have met you. I look forward to a long friendship —

Andre Marchionno
Lou Casamassa's Red Dragon Famora

To Gary Lee
Pleasure to meet you. I am Red Dragon Karate Kyodan of WKO former feather weight full contact champion, & bearer of state & national Karate & Kickboxing champions
Professional Martial artist
Joe Class

Dear Mr Gary Lee   8/14/02

Thank you so much for giving us this wonderful opportunity to be in part of great event.

Best Wishes,
Shime hiyuki

Lou Casamassa's
Red Dragon Karate, North Rancho

Garett Lee, Professor Gary Lee and
World Champion Chris Minshew

Made in the USA
Columbia, SC
25 August 2023